THE SAVVY ALLY

Praise for *The Savvy Ally*

"This book is long overdue, and I loved reading it! It is a call to action in a positive, optimistic, and engaging way—a masterful blend of information, personal stories, humor, and serious content. This is much more than just an informative book. It is designed to build skills that can be translated into ongoing, meaningful action. If you want to be an effective LBGTQ+ ally, buy this book. It won't just sit on your shelf. You'll use it every day!"—**Mike Streeter**, executive director, Workforce Diversity Network

"I love the compassionate sentiment that is weaved through this book that being an ally doesn't mean you have to be perfect; it means being able to acknowledge when a mistake is made and then trying your best to be better. If you truly want to be an ally, *The Savvy Ally* will lead the way through real-life examples, questions that make you go hmmm . . ., and 'what if' scenarios. Thank you, Jeannie Gainsburg, for supporting my ally journey!"—**Kimberly Braithwaite**, senior human resource manager, Barilla America Inc., and one of *Profiles in Diversity Journal*'s 2019 Women Worth Watching

"*The Savvy Ally* provides a successful foray into the confusing and ever-changing world of being an ally to the LGBTQ+ community. The thoughtful definitions, various analogies, and personal examples used to clarify issues are always helpful and often brilliant. Clearly, Gainsburg's many years of 'operating in solidarity with' the LGBTQ+ community have provided her with the necessary insight to create such a useful tool. I am grateful for such a perceptive and kindhearted book!"—**Matthew Burns**, dean of students, University of Rochester

"*The Savvy Ally* is a read for everyone. It is one of the best tutorials I've read that offers key insights into LGBTQ communities while offering practical guidance and action-oriented tips that will help allies become more culturally competent, respectful, and impactful in their interactions, both personally and in business."—**Joseph L. Searles Jr.**, corporate diversity relations director, Excellus BlueCross BlueShield

"*The Savvy Ally* is a book I will recommend again and again for its thoughtful approach to gaining knowledge, skill, and confidence. It's a much-needed tool in our box!"—**Kelly Clark**, director, Q Center, Binghamton University

THE SAVVY ALLY

A GUIDE FOR BECOMING A SKILLED LGBTQ+ ADVOCATE

Jeannie Gainsburg

ROWMAN & LITTLEFIELD
Lanham • Boulder • New York • London

Published by Rowman & Littlefield
An imprint of The Rowman & Littlefield Publishing Group, Inc.
4501 Forbes Boulevard, Suite 200, Lanham, Maryland 20706
www.rowman.com

6 Tinworth Street, London, SE11 5AL, United Kingdom

British Library Cataloguing in Publication Information Available

Library of Congress Cataloging-in-Publication Data Available

ISBN 9781538139400 (cloth)
ISBN 9781538136775 (paper)
ISBN 9781538136782 (ebook)

♾™ The paper used in this publication meets the minimum requirements of American National Standard for Information Sciences—Permanence of Paper for Printed Library Materials, ANSI/NISO Z39.48-1992.

To Scott Fearing,
for seeing and believing in the educator in me
long before I ever did

savvy [sav-ee] adj., experienced, knowledgeable, and well-informed

CONTENTS

PROLOGUE

They always say time changes things, but you actually have to change them yourself.

—Andy Warhol

For my fortieth birthday my husband gave me a book that changed my life. Up until that point I believed in LGBTQ+[1] equity and inclusion, but I hadn't done a thing to help create a more inclusive world. In February 2003, inspired by that book, I launched myself into a career as an ally[2] to the LGBTQ+ communities. Here is a brief summary of my life before, during, and after I read that book—and why I became motivated to write this one.

I grew up in New Jersey without any out LGBTQ+ friends or family members. I would later discover that I'd had plenty of LGBTQ+ friends—I just didn't know it. Despite this dearth of out and authentic LGBTQ+ people in my early life, the word *gay* wasn't avoided or considered naughty in my childhood home.

When I was ten, my mother leaned across the table at Serendipity, a restaurant in Manhattan, and said to me, "Did you know that all of the waiters here are gay?" My conclusion: Gay men are nice, clean, polite people who bring you fantastic food. These were clearly superior human beings.

At age fourteen, I was an avid fan of the TV sitcom *Soap*. Billy Crystal stole the show as Jodie, a bright, funny gay man who was one of the first-ever out and proud LGBTQ+ characters on television.

A few years ago I discovered evidence that my early environment had made me a tolerant child. While cleaning out my childhood desk, I found a note that I had passed in eighth grade science class (circa 1977) with my best friend; in it, we were discussing gay people. My friend argued that gay people were "gross." I countered with this thorough and articulate rebuttal: "What is your problem? Live and let live!"

Finding evidence that as a young teen in the 1970s I'd had a very chill attitude about gay people made me incredibly happy, but I certainly was no ally at that point. As a teenager, I couldn't understand why folks got their knickers in a knot over whom people loved, but I hadn't done anything to promote inclusion, understanding, and acceptance. I didn't know the word *ally* and I didn't know that, as someone who had no connection to the LGBTQ+ communities, there could be a role for me in supporting them. My budding passion and ally efforts would lie dormant for another quarter of a century.

All sorts of events related to the LGBTQ+ communities were brewing as I approached my fortieth birthday. Marriage equality was newly being discussed in the media. James Dale lost his lawsuit against the Boy Scouts of America, allowing the organization to legally continue to discriminate against gay scout leaders. My young children had started school, and I was disheartened to find that gay slurs were still extremely prevalent among elementary school children.

Then one night, I was in bed reading the book my husband had given me for my fortieth birthday: *Not for Ourselves Alone*. It's the companion book to the Ken Burns documentary on the battle to secure the right to vote for women in the United States. I was awed, thankful, and inspired by the amazing women who had gone before me and fought for my right to vote. I was doing something that I often find myself doing when I read history: I was imagining myself back in that time period and wondering how I would have behaved if I had lived then, and I had convinced myself that I would have fought alongside Susan B. Anthony and Elizabeth Cady Stanton.

Suddenly it hit me: What a hypocrite I was being! Here I was fantasizing about how I would have behaved more than a hundred years ago, while social justice battles were happening right now, in my own lifetime, and I was sitting them out! I thought to myself, "What will I tell my grandchildren if they ever ask me if I was involved in the fight for LGBTQ+ rights? When I reflect back on my life will I know that I have left the world a better place? How have I gotten so caught up in my daily life that I have lost track of the big picture?"

The next morning I looked up the word *gay* in the phone book (yes, I really did), found our local LGBTQ+ center, and called to ask if I could volunteer. I began my volunteer work by answering phones at the office and training to be a public speaker. I knew almost nothing about the LGBTQ+ communities, and I messed up frequently with my language and assumptions. The center's staff and volunteers were very welcoming, patient, and forgiving of my blunders, but I wished I had a guidebook to tell me what to say and what not to say, with concrete tips about what I could actually do to make the world a more inclusive place. That book didn't exist.

I volunteered at the center for three years. During that time I learned the word *ally* within the framework of social justice work. I now had an identity within the LGBTQ+ movement, which also meant that there was a place and a role for me! I was told repeatedly that my voice as an ally was incredibly important. My new volunteer work was truly life changing. It launched me into a career as an active ally.

In 2006 I was hired as the center's education and outreach coordinator. In 2013 I was promoted to education director, a role I held for more than five years. Since that first phone call I have met the most amazing people, learned so much about the LGBTQ+ communities and myself, and come to understand the many gifts I can give back to a group of people who have welcomed me with open arms.

This book, *The Savvy Ally*, is the book I wanted and needed when I first began my work as an ally. It is with so much appreciation and gratitude to the many people who encouraged, educated, and supported me that I now am able to offer it as a guide for others on their journey.

NOTES

1. A definition of *LGBTQ+* coming up in chapter 2. Jump ahead if you'd like it now.
2. A definition of *ally* coming up in chapter 1. Check it out early if that's helpful to you.

GETTING STARTED

How wonderful it is that nobody need wait a single moment before starting to improve the world.

—Anne Frank

THANK YOU

Ibegin my book with a heartfelt thank-you. The world needs more allies. Whether you are already fired up about being an ally to the LGBTQ+ communities and are currently out there doing ally stuff or you are just a little ally-curious, thank you for picking up this book and for your interest in creating a more equitable, safe, and inclusive world.

WHAT YOU CAN EXPECT FROM THIS BOOK

This book is focused on *how* to be an ally to the LGBTQ+ communities, not *why* to be an ally. There are many great books, movies, videos, and blogs out there that focus on the realities of living in our world as an LGBTQ+ person, the history of LGBTQ+ discrimination, and why allies are so important. They have been created with the purpose of motivating non-LGBTQ+ individuals to get involved. This book is not one of them. If you picked up this book, it's my hope that you are already on board with the idea that the world needs to be more LGBTQ+ inclusive and you want to know how you can help.

This book is a collection of the tools and skills that I have discovered over the past fifteen years to be most useful in being an ally to the LGBTQ+ communities. It includes pointers for having respectful and effective conversations, the most common places that allies get tripped up or stuck, and best-practice solutions for creating spaces that are LGBTQ+ inclusive. The book is divided into four main sections dealing with the following topics: (1) becoming knowledgeable allies, (2) building skills for having respectful conversations, (3) taking action to create more LGBTQ+ inclusive spaces, and (4) allying responsibly. My goal in writing this book is to create allies who are more active, who are kind to themselves, and who find ways to make allyship a sustainable part of their everyday life, not a frenzied burst of action followed by exhaustion or disillusionment. This book helps you navigate an often confusing and intimidating world of identities and terms and offers suggestions for creating positive change with your words and actions. It's not as daunting as it may seem. You've got this!

DEFINING ALLY BROADLY

An ally is a person who is not a part of a particular marginalized group but who stands up for and advocates for the rights of people in that group. Typically when we see the word *ally* in the context of LGBTQ+ advocacy, we think only of the person who is straight (i.e., heterosexual) and not transgender. However, we *all* can be LGBTQ+ allies, even if we are a part of the LGBTQ+ communities. If you are a lesbian, you can be an ally to the bisexual/pansexual communities. If you are a white transgender woman, you can support and advocate for transgender women of color.

One of my favorite post-training evaluation comments that I often receive from LGBTQ+ participants is: "Wow! I learned so much about the LGBTQ+ communities! I didn't know how much I didn't know!" You may be an expert on your own identity and community and yet know very little about others under the LGBTQ+ umbrella or how to be an ally to other communities. This book is for us all.

BRINGING MY FRIENDS ALONG FOR THE RIDE

Throughout my ally journey, LGBTQ+ community members and other allies generously shared their stories and experiences with me to help me understand concepts. With their permission, I have included quotes, stories, and experiences from my friends and colleagues to help bring concepts to light with voices from the LGBTQ+ and allied communities. When they desired it, I have honored these people by using their real names; I have used aliases for those who preferred anonymity. Thank you to all who have shared your personal experiences. You have made this book explode with personality, warmth, and humanity. It feels so right and so good to bring you all along with me for the ride.

PRACTICE MAKES PRETTY DARN GOOD

This book is not about how to be a perfect ally; it's about how to be a pretty darn good one. In an interview with *VolleyballUSA* magazine, three-time Olympic gold medalist Karch Kiraly advises: "Focus on just being good, play after play. Trying to be perfect often leads to poorer and less consistent performance."[1] Telling ourselves that we must perform perfectly sets us up to fail. It puts so much pressure on us that instead of elevating our game, it typically has the opposite effect.

My colleague Noah, a straight, white, transgender man, has gotten closer to becoming a perfect ally than anyone else I know. He is dedicated to social justice, he reads voraciously on the topic, he understands the nuances of advocacy work, and he is incredibly thoughtful and intentional in his language. He is my go-to guy whenever I need someone to discuss a social justice issue or concern. Here are his thoughts on perfect allies:

> I am far more interested in the Intentional Allies, folks who work hard toward the goal of advocating frequently but not every second of every day, than the Perfect Allies, folks who respond to every comment every time. I think living and acting intentionally is a far more manageable and sustainable experience.... Sustained 50 percent is better than a burst of 100 percent followed by burnout.

This book is about creating and maintaining pretty darn good allies by embracing our vulnerability, forgiving ourselves when we mess up, and working to be better.

THE POWER OF THE ALLY

Social justice movements need allies. Our numbers alone can help shift cultural norms and public perceptions of marginalized groups. But allies offer more than just bodies. Here are some of the valuable gifts that allies bring to social justice movements.

Allies Can Help Validate a Cause

You may be reading this book because you have an LGBTQ+ child, parent, or friend, and that's wonderful. I applaud you for seeking more ways to support them. The best-known ally organization in the nation is PFLAG, which was started by a gay man's mom. I don't have an LGBTQ+ child, and at the time that I began my work as a volunteer, I didn't have any local LGBTQ+ friends or acquaintances either. Because of this, many people asked me why I was getting involved. Think for a moment about the powerful statement made by this question. The implication is that no one would be involved in a particular social justice issue if it weren't about themselves, their family members, or their friends. Initially I was concerned that I wouldn't be welcome because I didn't have an LGBTQ+ family member. In the end, I found great value in sharing that I did not, as a way of validating the fight for LGBTQ+ equity and inclusion on its own merits.

Allies Can Be a Cultural Bridge

Because allies are not a part of the marginalized group, they often have a keen understanding of the myths, stereotypes, misunderstandings, and fears that get in the way of acceptance and that hold people back from getting involved (e.g., unflattering and inaccurate media portrayals of LGBTQ+ people, no personal connections to the LGBTQ+ communities, and the fear of saying something offensive). These obstacles may be the very same things that initially held us back in our own journey as allies. But the more we learn about LGBTQ+ individuals and communities, the better we become at changing hearts and minds outside those communities. We can help to bridge the gap between these two worlds and aid in understanding and communication.

Allies Can Be Possibility Models

The wonderful Laverne Cox, transgender advocate, actress, and star of the show *Orange Is the New Black*, came up with the phrase "possibility model." In an interview with *Radio Times*, she said, "I hate the term 'role model.' It's presumptuous to think that anyone should model their life after you, but I do like the term 'possibility model.'"[2]

I love this sentiment. One of the most amazing things I am able to do through my work is to be a possibility model for others. I was pleasantly surprised to find out how many ally wannabes there were in my midst. When I began talking about the work I was doing, I discovered that many of my friends and acquaintances were also fully on board with LGBTQ+ rights and inclusion and just didn't know what needed to be done or how to get involved. One of the projects I took on for our center was facilitating our bike ride fundraiser. Through this ride I assembled an army of allies. They were able to access communities previously unreached by LGBTQ+ advocates and talk about why they rode.

Allies Can Get Special Access

Because I am not a part of the LGBTQ+ communities, part of my growth as an ally was learning to navigate conversations about my identity and understanding when it was and when it wasn't important to share it. It became apparent early on that others often assumed that I was a lesbian. (Not shocking. I worked for an LGBTQ+ center and I wore comfortable shoes.)

FUN FACT

You can't really identify a lesbian by her shoes. (See chapter 6 on gaydar.)

Well, I wasn't a lesbian and I didn't "become" one either. Fifteen years working at an LGBTQ+ center and I didn't "catch the gay." I am living proof that it's not contagious. (Yes, that's a joke.) Often it was easier and more comfortable to simply let people assume that I was a member of the LGBTQ+ communities. However, there were many times when my voice as an ally was critical.

I learned that because of my identity as an ally, I have access to systems of power and communities of people that LGBTQ+ people often don't. Due to homophobia, biphobia, transphobia, and the fact that I am perceived as less threatening when I disclose that I am not LGBTQ+, I am able to have conversations around social change with people and in places that my LGBTQ+ friends cannot. I can wallow in this pitiful situation or I can view it as an opportunity to give something back to a community of people who have welcomed me with open arms. I choose the latter.

WHAT'S YOUR STORY?

As I mentioned earlier, this book isn't about why you should be an ally; it's about how to be an ally. The rest of this book will be focused on actions for helping to make the world a better and more inclusive place. However, I always get the "why" questions as I do this work, and I suspect you do (or you will) as well. Why are you so passionate? Why *this* social justice issue? Why are LGBTQ+ rights so important to you? Your responses to these questions can be a powerful tool for creating change and I encourage you to think about your answers. Here's one of mine.

I once asked my grandmother how the Holocaust happened. She was an elderly Jewish woman, and I thought she would be able to explain it to me. I wanted to know the details, like why the Jewish people didn't run, hide, or rip the Star of David from their clothing. But my grandmother had grown up in Brooklyn, and she couldn't explain it to me any better than the history books could.

It wasn't until I read *Schindler's List* that I began to understand the process of systematic oppression that had taken place: starting with the name-calling and scapegoating, moving gradually into discrimination and segregation, and on to acts of violence and eventually to genocide.

For many people the Holocaust must feel like ancient history. But for others—like me, in my fifties—it was shockingly recent. After hiding in a friend's attic for more than two years, Anne Frank was killed a mere eighteen years before I was born.

One of my biggest fears is that I *will* be able to explain to my grandchildren exactly how something like this could happen. How first we allowed doctors to refuse care to LGBTQ+ people because it went against their religious beliefs. How we then removed safe access to bathrooms and other facilities for transgender people. How there were mass shootings in LGBTQ+ spaces, until, finally, I had people hiding in *my* attic.

I refuse to allow this to become my future story. It's why I do the work that I do. It's why I wrote this book. Allies are a mighty and necessary force for any social justice movement. If you are inspired to be a part of that force, or you are already, I hope this book will give you tools for your adventure. If the fire to create change is not yet burning within you, I am honored that you are giving me the opportunity to light the match.

NOTES

1. Don Patterson, "40 Keys to Volleyball Greatness," *VolleyballUSA* (summer 2014): 39.

2. "*Orange Is the New Black*'s Wonder Woman Laverne Cox on Being a Transgender Trailblazer," *RadioTimes*, July 26, 2015, https://www.radiotimes.com/news/2015-07-26/orange-is-the-new-blacks-wonder-woman-laverne-cox-on-being-a-transgender-trailblazer/.

Part I

BECOMING KNOWLEDGEABLE ALLIES

THE GLOSSARY
IS AT THE BACK

It's "I-dentity" not "YOU-dentity." Respect people's right to self-define.

—Robyn Ochs

I have added a glossary of some of the basic LGBTQ+ terms at the back of this book for you to use as a reference. Identities are incredibly important, and I will share more about why that is later in this chapter. However, I have found that focusing too heavily on a large glossary of terms has the opposite effect than one might hope. People can get so intimidated by the enormous number of terms and identities that instead of having conversations, they are completely silenced by their fear that they are accidentally going to say something wrong, outdated, or insulting.

Instead, in this book, I am choosing to share tips on how to navigate respectful conversations with LGBTQ+ individuals even if you don't know or remember *any* of the proper terms. So when you have a moment, feel free to take a look at the basic glossary of LGBTQ+ terms and identities that I have provided at the back. Read the warning first and then proceed with caution. Do become familiar with the words. Do not walk through the world with your glossary in hand, labeling people.

With all of that said, there are three terms I would like to focus on in this chapter in order to ensure we are all on the same page so you can get the most out of this book. They are *cisgender*, *LGBTQ+*, and *queer*.

CISGENDER

The first term is one I already had to dance around in chapter 1, so it's definitely time to define it. This word is an excellent one to add to your vocabulary, if it's not there already. From here on I use it throughout the book. The word is *cisgender*. A cisgender person is an individual whose sex assigned at birth matches their gender identity, or who they know themselves to be. In other words, if the doctor or midwife said, "It's a girl!" when you arrived on the planet and as you grew that fit for you—most likely so well you never even thought about whether it fit or not—you are cisgender. It's a word that means "not transgender."

For those of you who are word nerds and get excited by etymology, the prefixes *cis* and *trans* originally come from Latin. *Cis* means "on this side of" and *trans* means "across" or "on the far side." So a very simplified way of thinking about this is if the sex you were assigned at birth matches or is on the same side as your gender identity, you are cisgender. If these things do not match or are across from each other, you are trans.

LGBTQ+

You have probably seen many versions of the LGBTQ+ initialism. Here is a brief history of my experience with the initialism and why I have chosen to use *LGBTQ+* in this book.

At the time of this book's publication, in my current location in Upstate New York, the full initialism most often being used is LGBTQQIAA2SPP. This stands for "lesbian, gay, bisexual, transgender, queer, questioning, intersex, asexual, ally, Two-Spirit, pansexual, and polyamorous." (If you are unfamiliar with any of these identities, please take a look at that glossary at the back of the book.) The reality is that the LGBTQQIAA2SPP initialism is large, somewhat intimidating, and—most importantly—ever changing. In addition, what nonprofit LGBTQ+ center can afford the ink to print that whole thing out on its brochures? (Yes, that's also a joke.) The "+" was created not to devalue the identities that come after the "Q" but to make the initialism more user-friendly and always relevant. LGBTQ+ stands for lesbian, gay, bisexual, transgender, queer/questioning, plus so much more!

Here is the history of the progression of the commonly used initialism during my work as an ally over the past fifteen years. When I first started in 2003, the initialism being used most often was GLBT. A few years later it had changed to

LGBT. I believe the thinking around this was, "Hey! Why do men always get listed first? Let's put women first for a change." Which is cool. If I ran the world, I would change up the order of the letters every five years or so, just to keep it fair: "Congratulations to our bisexual friends! It's your turn at the front!"

About five or six years later, around 2013, many organizations had changed the initialism on their websites and literature to LGBTQ in an attempt to be even more inclusive. The Q can stand for *questioning*, or *queer*, or both.

The word *questioning* is often included in the initialism to help us remember and embrace the fact that for many people, identity is ever changing. Understanding who we are and defining our attractions can be a long process and may change over time. Many social and support groups include the word *questioning* in the list of people who are welcome to join them so that individuals know they can attend the group even if they haven't got it all figured out yet.

In 2018 our local agency made the excellent decision to change the initialism used on its website and all materials to LGBTQ+. I notice that many other agencies have done the same. I have chosen to use it throughout my book in an effort to be as inclusive as possible.

QUEER

Historically the word *queer* was used in an offensive and hurtful way, and there are folks who will never feel comfortable using it. Typically, these tend to be older folks who experienced the use of the word *queer* in a derogatory way, but sometimes it's younger folks too. Some LGBTQ+ people, however, have reclaimed this word and love it! The word *queer* can be used as an identity to define a person's orientation, gender, or both. So basically, anyone who is not straight and cisgender might embrace this term.

Reasons I have heard that explain why an individual might refer to themselves as *queer* include:

- A person may be several of the identities in the LGBTQ+ initialism, so no one letter or single identity word works for them. For example, they may be a bisexual, polyamorous trans woman.
- A person might use the term *queer* because, although they are proud to be a part of the community, they don't feel like they should have to identify as one or several of the letters.
- A person might find that their identities are ever changing and evolving.

POP QUIZ

Choose all that apply.

A. *Queer* is an offensive word that historically was used against LGBTQ+ people and should never be used.
B. Some people love the word *queer* and others hate it. Proceed with caution.
C. *Queer* is a word that has been reclaimed by the LGBTQ+ communities and is now okay to use (e.g., queer studies and *Queer Eye for the Straight Guy*).

Answer: B

We have no way of knowing how someone feels about the word *queer* unless we ask. It's a hot topic. If you get a bunch of LGBTQ+ people in a room and ask them how they feel about the word, you could be there for months listening to the answers. A best-practice tip for allies is to avoid using the word unless you hear someone embracing it as their identity word.

So how do we navigate a world where people have such different opinions about the word *queer*? How do we know who loves the word and who hates it? How can we have conversations with LGBTQ+ people without giving offense? We will get to that in chapter 5.

WHY DO THERE HAVE TO BE SO MANY IDENTITIES?

A very common question is: "Why do we need all of these identities? Can't we just all be human?" I do love the sentiment behind this question, and typically it is asked by people who are coming from a really good and respectful place. But unfortunately, it's just not that simple. Understanding and being able to explain why there need to be so many identities is a great task for a savvy ally!

So let's begin dissecting this question by thinking about who is asking it. Typically this question comes from someone who has already figured out their identity or identities and has their word or words locked in place. Often, if the asker is straight and cisgender, they never even had to think about the fact that their identity words were readily accessible, because their identity matched societal expectations.

Interestingly, this question can and does also come from folks within the LGBTQ+ communities. A young, straight trans man who became one of our agency's very best facilitators admits that, before he started his work as an LGBTQ+ educator, he also used to ask this question. He looked at relatively new identity words like *genderqueer, pansexual, nonbinary,* and *agender* and thought, "Really? Enough already! This is getting ridiculous." He now understands that, because he had found his identity words (*straight* and *transgender*), his hunt was over. These words fit for him, and in general, they are understood and accepted words in the English language. He was now in a place of relative comfort with his identity words as he observed others still seeking their words. And he thought to himself, "Can't we stop already with all of these new words?"

Every single word was once new. Words are created when there is a need. The word *cisgender,* which I defined above, is a great example. Why did we need a word that meant *not transgender*? Well, first of all, saying, "I'm a straight, nontransgender ally" is clunky. More importantly, before we had a term that meant *not transgender,* people often used words like *normal*—as in, "I'm not transgender. I'm normal," which is pretty darn offensive.

Here is the story of someone whose identity word had not yet been created in her language. Dee is a transgender woman who grew up in the Philippines. She knew from an early age that she felt different, but she wasn't sure why. As she looked out into the world to see if there was anyone else like her and to try and find out who she was, she landed on the word *bakla.* It was the only word she could find in her language. Dee told me that *bakla* was a term used for a person who was identified male at birth but expressed themselves in a very feminine manner. There were no separate Filipino words for a gay man, a transgender woman, and a cross-dressing man; they all just got lumped together and labeled *bakla.* So the understanding was that a cisgender gay man was the same as trans woman. What this meant for Dee was that she hung out at school with the gay guys and got labeled by others as *bakla,* but the term never really fit for her. When she was introduced to the English word *transgender,* a lightbulb went off in her head—Dee had found her identity word!

According to trans advocate Alex Myers, "Adding more labels to the acronym isn't about making sure all the snowflakes know they are special. These labels save lives. These labels create a powerful sense of understanding and self-acceptance. The fact that the acronym has become a target for mockery only indicates the amount of work that still needs to be done around LGBTQIA+ civil rights."[1]

I hope I live to see a time when we all can just identify as human, but the reality is that we have a lot more work to do before we get there. We will know we're there when legal rights and protections are in place for everyone; when

> **FUN FACT**
>
> Many people refer to the LGBTQ+ abbreviation as an acronym. However, an acronym is an invented word that has been created using the letters in the abbreviation, like MADD (Mothers Against Drunk Driving) or DARE (Drug Abuse Resistance Education). LGBTQ+ is actually an initialism because each letter is stated individually.

people stop making assumptions that everyone is straight and cisgender; when it's as easy for someone to come out as any of the identities under the LGBTQ+ umbrella as it was for me to come out as a straight, cisgender person; and when no one gives a rat's tushie how anyone else identifies. We are definitely not there yet. There's lots more savvy ally work to be done.

NOTE

1. Alex Myers, "Why We Need More Queer Identity Labels, Not Fewer," *Slate*, January 16, 2018, https://slate.com/human-interest/2018/01/lgbtq-people-need-more-labels-not-fewer.html.

COMING OUT AS LGBTQ+

*I've endured years of misery and gone to enormous lengths
to live a lie. I was certain that my world would fall apart if
anyone knew. And yet when I acknowledged my sexuality I felt
whole for the first time.*

—Jason Collins

WHY THE BIG REVEAL?

"**M**om, Dad . . . please sit down. I've got something to tell you. I know this is going to come as a surprise, but for a long time now I have known something about myself and it's time that I shared it with you. . . . I'm, um . . . straight." Nope. It never happens. Straight and cisgender people don't have to come out. They are pretty much just out.

Let's think about that for a moment. Why is that? Straight and cisgender people don't have to come out because we meet all of the expectations of who we "should" be. (Please notice the quotation marks here.) I was assigned female at birth and that fit for me. I never questioned it. My parents expected me to grow up to be straight and I did. How do I know that my parents expected me to grow up to be straight? Because everything I ever heard from them regarding a future partner (boyfriend/husband) and every book they ever read to me was heterosexually oriented. Straight/cisgender people don't ever have to come out because our orientation and gender are correctly assumed; we have met expectations and we are on the "right" course.

What this means for our LGBTQ+ friends, of course, is that unless they have grown up in a completely isolated, super-inclusive bubble—where they didn't go to school, had no contact with other children, weren't a part of any faith community, didn't play on any sports teams, didn't watch popular movies, and didn't read popular books—they have gotten the impression, as they figured out their identities, that they were on the "wrong" course.

As the education director at the LGBTQ+ center where I worked, I was in charge of training all of our volunteer Speakers Bureau members. Therefore, I had the privilege of hearing hundreds of coming-out stories. One of the things that struck me was that every speaker had an extremely difficult time coming out to their parents. This was true even when their stories involved parents who constantly let their child know that they would be loved no matter what, who made a point of talking positively about LGBTQ+ people, and who had LGBTQ+ friends who were welcomed into their homes. What these speakers shared with me was that the negative messages they received about being LGBTQ+ from the outside world were much stronger than the positive messages they were getting inside of their homes.

Since the legislation of marriage equality on a national level, I find that people often believe that we are now in a pretty good place in our country regarding LGBTQ+ rights, inclusion, and acceptance, and that our work is done. It's not.

THE COMING-OUT PROCESS

Our society's limited expectations of and assumptions about who people are and who they should be gives LGBTQ+ people two choices that they must constantly make as they go about their daily business: They must either come out or live a lie. Please bear with me while I repeat that; I don't want anyone to miss it: Our society forces LGBTQ+ people to constantly either come out or lie. Most LGBTQ+ people do not come out to shock people or because they want to be "in your face" with their sexuality. They come out because we as a society have a limited and narrow view of who people are and who they should be, and LGBTQ+ people do not fit those expectations. This is not because there is a problem with LGBTQ+ people. This is because there is a problem with our society.

What does it look like when you don't fit into society's expected identity boxes? How do you come to terms with that and lead a healthy and happy life? It's a process. Having a basic understanding of that process is essential for allies.

It helps us understand why sometimes anger is directed toward straight, cisgender people for no apparent reason at all; why having positive LGBTQ+ role models is so critical; why an LGBTQ+ person might tell hurtful gay jokes; and why being supportive and kind when someone comes out to you is so very important.

In order to understand the process, we are going to look at a developmental model of coming out. There are many models out there in the world, but one of the first, developed in 1979 by therapist Vivienne Cass,[1] is the model that most of the others have sprung from.

As is true with all developmental models, it will ring true for some people and it will not for others, so please understand that I am not claiming that all LGBTQ+ individuals feel this model resonates with them. It doesn't. However, my experience has been that this model resonates with a heck of a lot of LGBTQ+ people and that it's a very useful tool for understanding.

Here is my personal synopsis of the six stages of coming out as LGBTQ+, adapted from Cass's model, followed by an example of how a person might behave in each of the stages.

Identity Confusion

Identity confusion is the stage where the individual feels different. They may not even be thinking along the lines of LGBTQ+ identities yet. They just know that they are not like the others. The big question is, "Who am I?"

Identity Comparison

In the identity comparison stage the person asks themselves, "Might I be [gay, lesbian, transgender, etc.]?" and begins to look out into the world and compare themselves to what they know about these people.

Remember when professional basketball player Jason Collins came out as gay? There was a great deal of pushback from people who wondered, "Why did he have to come out? Couldn't he just be a basketball player? Why is his sexual orientation important?" The identity comparison stage is why having a professional athlete like Collins publicly come out is so important.

Think about a teenage boy in this stage trying to figure out if he might be gay. He looks out into the world to see what it means to be a gay man, what that looks like, and how it's received. If he looks out and he only sees negative images and stereotypes of gay men—think Axel Foley as the diseased Ramon in *Beverly Hills Cop* or Mr. Antolini, Holden Caulfield's predatory teacher in *The Catcher in the Rye*—he will typically think one of two things. He might think, "That's not me," in which case he will go back into the identity confusion stage and wonder, "If I'm not gay, why do I feel so different?" He might also think, "I'm pretty sure I am gay, but being gay is clearly bad. I am never telling anyone." And he will move into the stage of identity tolerance, feeling pretty crummy about who he is.

Now let's think about what happens if he looks out into the world and he sees the out gay athlete Jason Collins or the out gay actor Neil Patrick Harris. Truth be told, because of all those societal expectations that he should be straight, he probably is still not jumping up and down with glee, but his journey toward self-acceptance is likely to be a lot smoother. With powerful, bright, and healthy gay role models like Collins and Harris, and better media portrayal of gay men, like Lieutenant Sulu in the *Star Trek* reboot, he is more likely to move rapidly through this stage of identity comparison, and also through the next stage of identity tolerance.

Identity Tolerance

The word *tolerance* gets thrown around a lot in social justice circles and is often confused with *acceptance*, but the two are actually pretty different. We tolerate things that we dislike but have no control over, like traffic or a bad cold. Tolerating your identity is not a good or healthy place to be. The identity tolerance stage is when the person has come out to themselves but is unlikely to come out to others. They may think of their identity as their dirty little

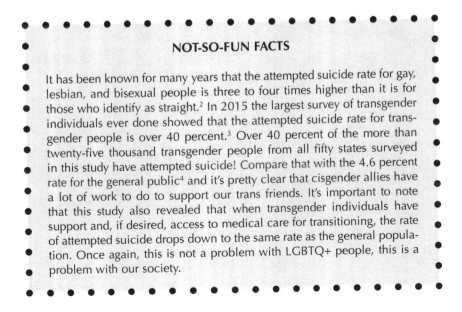

NOT-SO-FUN FACTS

It has been known for many years that the attempted suicide rate for gay, lesbian, and bisexual people is three to four times higher than it is for those who identify as straight.[2] In 2015 the largest survey of transgender individuals ever done showed that the attempted suicide rate for transgender people is over 40 percent.[3] Over 40 percent of the more than twenty-five thousand transgender people from all fifty states surveyed in this study have attempted suicide! Compare that with the 4.6 percent rate for the general public[4] and it's pretty clear that cisgender allies have a lot of work to do to support our trans friends. It's important to note that this study also revealed that when transgender individuals have support and, if desired, access to medical care for transitioning, the rate of attempted suicide drops down to the same rate as the general population. Once again, this is not a problem with LGBTQ+ people, this is a problem with our society.

secret that nobody else ever needs to know. This is the stage where suicidal ideation and suicide attempts are likeliest.

Identity Acceptance

In the stage of identity acceptance, the individual begins to realize that they are not the only LGBTQ+ person in the world and that they are going to be okay. This is the stage where many people begin to seek out others like themselves and make their first attempts at coming out. They may come out to a total stranger to test the waters because it feels safer, or they may come out to a trusted friend or family member. (Perhaps one who is wearing a big rainbow ally pin! Just sayin'.) How their first coming-out reveal is received may affect whether they move into identity pride, hang out in identity acceptance, or move back into identity tolerance.

Identity Pride

Identity pride is the stage I like to call the loud and proud stage. People on the outside looking in often describe people in this stage as obnoxious, aggressive, angry, or over the top. It's important for allies to understand where these loud and proud behaviors and attitudes are coming from and to appreciate the experience that the person has survived.

Identity pride is the stage where the person is finally out to the world and it feels *so* good! In many cases it means that the person has come out to some folks during the identity acceptance stage and the world has not ended. In fact, they may have been surprised by the support they received. In the identity acceptance stage they may have met other supportive LGBTQ+ people. Now, in the identity pride stage, they are sloughing off that oppressive cloak of self-hatred, self-doubt, and fear, and stepping out into the world as their authentic, out and proud selves. The aggression and anger that sometimes comes with this stage stems from having had to lie for so long about who they are, an impulse to protect their new authentic selves, and a vow not to go back into the closet and hide who they are ever again.

A participant in one of my workshops had a lightbulb go off when I described the identity pride stage. She said, "Oh wow! This makes so much sense! I had a customer come into my shop recently and she said, 'I'm a lesbian. Okay? Do you have a problem with that? 'Cause if you have a problem with that I'll go somewhere else.' And I thought to myself, 'What the heck? Did I do something to make her feel unsafe or unwelcome?' This makes total sense now!"

For a person in the identity pride stage, their identity as LGBTQ+ is likely to be at the forefront of all of their other identities. They may have fewer straight/cisgender friends during this time. They may be intolerant of LGBTQ+ people who are not living out and authentically. If they are a student, every writing assignment is likely to be about their LGBTQ+ identity. If they are in the workplace, they may suddenly add a pride flag to their cubicle. Typically, you know when someone is in the stage of identity pride: You can see the rainbows flowing from the back of their heads.

Identity Synthesis

With time, patience, love, and support, most LGBTQ+ individuals will move into the stage of identity synthesis. In this stage they are, of course, still proud to be LGBTQ+, but it's not everything they are about. I have a friend who says that when he was in the identity pride stage he was a Capital-G Gay professor. Now in the stage of identity synthesis, he is gay, a professor, a father, a dog owner, a basketball player, a wine enthusiast, etc. Being gay is just a part of who he is.

Is there still anger and aggression in this final stage? There certainly can be—and for good reason. However, the anger is typically more appropriately focused on people who are being disrespectful or discriminatory, not on the entire straight/cisgender population.

In Summary

To sum things up, let's look at how differently an LGBTQ+ person might respond to a coworker's question, "Hey! I'm going to the Pride parade this Saturday. Anyone wanna come?" depending on where the LGBTQ+ person is in their process of coming out:

Identity Confusion: "I don't think so, thanks."
Identity Comparison: "I don't think so, thanks."
Identity Tolerance: "Seriously? No way! I'm no homo."
Identity Acceptance: "Um . . . I've got other plans on Saturday, but thanks for asking." (And then a text later in the day: "Actually, I would like to go with u to the parade. LOL")
Identity Pride: "Hells yeah!!! I'm pumped!!! I'm buying rainbow tutus for everyone!!!"
Identity Synthesis: "I'm pretty sure I can. Let me check with my partner and I'll let you know. Thanks."

FROM THEORY TO REALITY

What I've shared above is a theoretical developmental model. Now let's look at the realities of coming out in the real world. Typically, folks do not move seamlessly, in a completely linear fashion through the six stages of the Cass model to the final stage of identity synthesis, and then—*ding!*—they're done! The Cass model is a tool that can be helpful to understand the coming-out process, but when we look at people's real-life experiences, there are some key points to keep in mind.

Coming Out Is a Lifelong Process

Coming out for LGBTQ+ people is not a single event. Folks do not leap from the closet on their official coming-out day with Diana Ross's "I'm Coming Out" blasting in the background—"Ta-da! I'm out!"—never to return to the closet ever again. (I find this unfortunate, because that would be pretty fabulous.) Coming out is a lifelong process.

My friend Jonathan, a gay man, was buying flowers for his husband at the grocery store a few years ago. Very kindly, just making conversation, the cashier said, "Oh, those are beautiful. Are they for your wife?" Jonathan had just popped into the market to purchase flowers, and now he was faced with a decision about whether to come out to the cashier or not.

The decision to come out or not, at any given moment, depends on many factors, not the least of which is safety. Lesbian comedian Sabrina Matthews recalls one of these moments: "I remember flying through Dallas/Fort Worth Airport on National Coming Out Day with my National Coming Out Day tee shirt on because I'm proud . . . and my sweatshirt over that, because I'm smart."[5]

The idea that people can create safe and welcoming spaces with their language is an incredibly important one. As allies, we should strive to model inclusive language at all times and educate others on its importance. In chapter 5, we will look at language choices that won't force people into the come-out-or-lie position.

The Process Is Not Always Linear

Some folks find that they move in a very linear fashion through the six stages of the Cass model. Others jump around a bit, skip stages, go back, and generally travel through them like an Upstate New York driver in March, skidding and swerving down a pothole-filled street. People can actually move across several stages in the very same day. For example, let's think about a college student who is in the identity synthesis stage on campus. They are out to all their friends and they speak freely about their identity. Then they return home for Thanksgiving to a family that has indicated that being LGBTQ+ is not okay, and they slide back into the identity tolerance stage, hiding their identity and feeling unhappy about who they are. People may spend a lifetime jumping around in the different stages, depending on whom they are with and how open and accepting the environment feels.

It's So Much Fun, Some Folks Do It Twice!

Okay, I'm actually kidding about it being fun, but some folks definitely go through the process of coming out twice or even more times than that. I know several straight, transgender men who came out first as cisgender lesbians. Most of them didn't even know the word *transgender* at their first coming out, so they didn't have that identity word to latch on to. (Remember our earlier discussion about the importance of all of those identity words?) So as they began looking out into the world during the identity comparison stage, they grabbed hold of the term *lesbian*. They knew they were attracted to girls/women, and *lesbian* fit a lot better than *straight*. Many of these men got all the way into the identity pride stage before they heard the term *transgender*, met some transgender people, and eventually realized that the reason they felt so different wasn't their sexual orientation but instead their gender. Then they had to backtrack and come out again with their new identity as straight transgender men. My friend Sean, a bisexual trans man, who traveled a long, winding road of self-discovery around both his sexual orientation and gender, jokes about how at one point or another in his life, he was every single letter of the LGBTQ initialism.

It's Not Just for LGBTQ+ People

This developmental model was originally based on cisgender gay men and cisgender lesbian women. However, it resonates with lots of other folks both within the LGBTQ+ communities and outside of the LGBTQ+ communities.

My friend Todd is Deaf. His parents, wanting only what they felt was best for him, insisted that he learn to read lips and speak so that he could fit into the hearing world. He lived in a rural town, so he didn't know there was a Deaf community and, as a child, was never exposed to sign language. When he moved to Upstate New York, he found others like himself. He shared with me that he went through every one of the Cass model stages as a Deaf man. When he hit that pride stage he said that it felt so amazing to be with other people like himself, to find community and understanding, and to embrace American Sign Language (ASL) as his language. Hearing friends and coworkers, who did not understand this fantastic feeling of connection and community, felt that he had gotten a bit "aggressive" with the whole Deaf thing and that he needed to tone it down a bit. Todd was "flaunting" his Deafness. Sound familiar?

Even family members and friends of LGBTQ+ people find that this model rings true for them. My friend Wanda, a cisgender lesbian, grew up in Puerto Rico. When she was eighteen her mother woke her up at 5:00 one morning, handed her a plane ticket, and sent her to a mental health institution in New York to be "fixed." She didn't even get a chance to say good-bye to her siblings. After this incident, Wanda's mom went through a journey that involved lots of time, new information, and, finally, interactions with her daughter, who was clearly so much happier and healthier as an out lesbian. Wanda's mom moved slowly from the stages of confusion, comparison, and tolerance into the stage of acceptance of her daughter's identity. Several years later, Mom was in her pride stage, marching alongside her daughter in our local Pride parade! I believe she has toned it down a bit recently and is less likely to "flaunt" her pride for her daughter, but she still loves a good drag show. The first response from someone to whom a friend or family member has just come out is likely to be different from how they feel years, months, or possibly even days later. Friends and family members may need to go through their own coming-out process as supporters and allies.

Coming Out Is Not Always the Immediate Goal

I hope that someday we will live in a world where everyone can live authentically and be out in all aspects of their lives, but that's not the reality for many LGBTQ+ folks. Unfortunately, many people are in environments where it's not safe to come out. Therefore, we should not think of coming out as an absolute, essential, and immediate goal for everyone. If a young person comes to you, for example, and shares that they are thinking of coming out to their parents, consider asking the youth how their parents are likely to respond. If there is a reasonable chance that this youth will end up homeless or without any financial support, then perhaps coming out should not be the goal at that time. That conversation should wait until the youth is less dependent on their parents for basic needs or until the youth has a solid safety net and a support system in place.

WHAT TO SAY WHEN SOMEONE COMES OUT TO YOU

Coming out as LGBTQ+ is often scary, and it's a big deal. What does that mean, then, if someone comes out to you? Typically it means that this person trusts you immensely. It's a huge compliment. Therefore, a great thing to say, if you are so inclined, is, "Thank you." You might say, "Thank you for trusting me enough to let me know," or, "Thank you for caring about our relationship and for being so honest with me."

After thanking them, I would recommend mostly listening. Let them take the lead on what they want to talk about. They may, in fact, not want to talk about anything. It may just be a huge relief to tell someone and know that they are supported.

If there is an awkward silence you could throw in one or two of these comments as well:

"Congratulations! I'm so happy for you."
"I'm here for you."
"I just want you to know that nothing will change between us."
"This calls for a celebration! Can I take you out for a beer?"

It's also important to keep confidentiality in mind. Coming out is the LGBTQ+ person's job, not yours. You should *never* out the person to others. If it doesn't come up naturally in the coming-out conversation, you may want to say something like, "I want to be very careful that I keep this information confidential. Are you comfortable telling me who else knows?" If the individual has come out as transgender and is asking you to use a new name and pronoun, it is also critical to discuss when and where the new name and pronoun should be used. Sometimes people will ask close friends to support them and affirm their identity by using their new name and pronoun in private, but they will use their old name and pronoun in public with others because they are not ready to come out or they don't feel safe doing so. Getting clarity on how the person would like you to navigate those situations is important and shows how committed you are to supporting them and keeping them safe.

WHAT NOT TO SAY WHEN SOMEONE COMES OUT TO YOU

If someone comes out to you, do try to avoid asking, "Are you sure? Perhaps this is just a phase." Even if you truly think that this might just be a phase, saying it aloud is unlikely to be received well. If it *is* a phase, the person will figure it out in their own time. For now it's their reality and it should be respected. If it's not a phase, you are at risk of really pissing them off.

Another question to avoid asking is when they "decided" to be LGBTQ+. Just as I didn't choose or decide to be straight or cisgender, LGBTQ+ people don't choose their identities. A better question to ask is, "How long have you known this about yourself?"

A great point by Dannielle Owens-Reid and Kristin Russo, from their book *This Is a Book for Parents of Gay Kids*,[6] is to avoid saying "I always knew," even if you did. You may be pleased by your expert sleuthing, but keep it to yourself. Hearing that you knew already may make the person coming out to you feel foolish or cowardly for waiting so long, diminish the importance of the information they want to share with you, cause them to wonder what they did to make it so obvious, and make them worry that others can also tell.

Finally, you should also avoid asking questions about a person's anatomy or sexual behaviors. There is an interesting phenomenon that sometimes happens when people talk about LGBTQ+ individuals and the LGBTQ+ communities: Their heads go right to the person's body parts and/or what they are doing in the bedroom. Being LGBTQ+ is not a bedroom issue and it does not give us a free pass to ask invasive questions about someone's body or sex life. It's about being able to live authentically and safely in all aspects of life. So asking a gay man who has just come out to you, "Have you slept with a guy yet?" or asking a trans woman, "Are you planning on having surgery?" is not okay. Just because someone comes out to you does not mean that they are required to be an open book. If you're curious about what LGBTQ+ people actually do in the bedroom or what types of surgeries are available for transgender people, do some online research.

If someone comes out to you and you're not sure if a question is okay or not, the "switch it" technique is useful: Switch the person's LGBTQ+ identity for straight or cisgender and try the question again in your head. Is the question polite, supportive, or useful, or is it offensive, invasive, or motivated by curiosity? Never in my fifty-six years of living have I ever had anyone ask me, "Do you think being cisgender might just be a phase?" or, "How do you know you're straight if you've never slept with a woman?" Our society believes I am on the "right" course and therefore no one has ever questioned my sexual orientation or gender.

Another great thing to keep in mind that may help to steer you away from inappropriate questions is that sexual orientation and sexual behaviors are completely separate things. One has to do with whom we are attracted to and

POP QUIZ

What *do* LGBTQ+ people do in the bedroom?

A. Have sex
B. Read books
C. Sleep
D. Occasionally vacuum and change the sheets
E. All of the above

Answer: E

A friend of mine described a workshop he participated in once where everyone in the room got an index card. On one side they wrote down their sexual orientation and gender. On the other side, they wrote down a favorite sexual activity. They then put all of the cards on a table with the "sexual activity" side up. The facilitator asked the participants to look at the sexual activities and figure out who was gay, lesbian, bisexual, transgender, straight, and cisgender. Guess what happened? They couldn't do it. They had no idea. Humans can be very creative in the bedroom, and no one group has cornered the market on any one sexual activity. Are there straight couples who engage in anal sex? Yup. Are there gay couples who have never engaged in anal sex? Yup. It's disrespectful and inaccurate to make assumptions about or to define a group of people by what we think they are doing in the bedroom.

the other is what we actually do. Think about when you first knew whom you were attracted to. I had a pretty solid idea by the time I was in third grade. Was I having sex yet? No. I didn't need to have sex to know that my little nine-year-old heart went pitter-patter every time I looked at Danny Fox.

I often hear this comment from straight, cisgender people: "No one should be out in the workplace. That's not appropriate." Actually, the vast majority of straight, cisgender people are out in the workplace. They talk about the movie they saw over the weekend with their wife. They have a photo of their husband on their desk. They bring their girlfriend to the company's holiday party. This is what being out in the workplace looks like. Being out at work doesn't mean I am going to share with you the new sexual position my partner and I just discovered. An important role for allies is to help folks understand the difference between sexual orientation (which comes with us to work) and sexual behaviors (which do not).

FUTURE FANTASIES

I hope I live long enough to see the Cass model and other LGBTQ+ identity development models disappear. They won't be needed because our societal expectations will have shifted. Parents, teachers, friends, and faith leaders will read stories to children about all kinds of people and families, will use language that doesn't assume sexual orientation or gender, and will have no expectations about who a person is or who they will be. There will be no fear, shame, or despair for anyone as they figure out who they are and whom they are attracted to. LGBTQ+ centers will close down or become museums, and books like this one will no longer be needed. Students will read about conversion therapy (therapy aimed at turning gay people straight) and people like CeCe McDonald and Matthew Shepard in their history books and say, "Can you believe stuff like that used to happen back then?" (If you aren't familiar with CeCe McDonald or Matthew Shepard, there's some ally homework for you.) In this future world, it will be as easy to come out as LGBTQ+ as it was for me to come out as a straight cisgender person. The Cass model process will disappear not because we have fixed our LGBTQ+ people but because we have fixed our society.

NOTES

1. Vivienne Cass, "Homosexual Identity Formation: A Theoretical Model," *Journal of Homosexuality* 4, no. 3 (spring 1979): 219–235.

2. Laura Kann, Emily O'Malley Olsen, Tim McManus, et al., "Sexual Identity, Sex of Sexual Contacts, and Health-Related Behaviors among Students in Grades 9–12—United States and Selected Sites, 2015," *Center for Disease Control and Prevention Morbidity and Mortality Weekly Report, Surveillance Summaries* 65, no. 9 (August 12, 2016): 19–22.

3. S. E. James, J. L. Herman, S. Rankin, et al., *The Report of the 2015 U.S. Transgender Survey* (Washington, DC: National Center for Transgender Equality, 2016), https://transequality.org/sites/default/files/docs/usts/USTS-Full-Report-Dec17.pdf.

4. Ibid.

5. Rich Tackenberg (director), *Coming Out Party* (Studio City, CA: Ariztical Entertainment, 2003), DVD.

6. Dannielle Owens-Reid and Kristin Russo, *This Is a Book for Parents of Gay Kids* (San Francisco: Chronicle Books, 2014).

ORIENTATIONS, IDENTITIES, BEHAVIORS-OH MY!

Binaries are for computers.

Anonymous

If you have ever asked (or, let's face it, been too embarrassed to ask):

"What the heck does nonbinary mean?"
"Can transgender people also be gay?"
"How can I tell if someone is gay?"
"How can someone identify as asexual but still have sex?"

then this is the chapter for you. In this chapter we will take a look at the various components that are part of who we are as sexual and gendered beings and answer these and many other questions that can be incredibly confusing.

Whether we have had to think long and hard about our sexuality, our gender, and our identities (as have most LGBTQ+ folks) or we have given very little thought to these things because we never had to (as is the case with most straight, cisgender people), we are all represented on the diagram of the components of sex, gender, and sexuality that we are about to discuss. This diagram shows the five components that make up our sexual and gendered selves: biological sex, gender identity, gender expression, attraction, and intimate behaviors.[1] Even though only three categories are depicted for each of the five components, please think of each component as a continuum with billions of people represented at various points all over the spectrum.

Toward the end of this chapter, for your reading pleasure, I will map myself out using this diagram. Think about where you fall on each component and map yourself out too. I encourage you to do this either in private or, for the more adventurous, perhaps at the dinner table during your next big family gathering.

A BASIC DIAGRAM OF THE COMPONENTS OF SEX, GENDER, AND SEXUALITY

Biological Sex

The first component that makes up human sex, gender, and sexuality is biological sex. Our biological sex has to do with our reproductive system, hormones, chromosomes, genitalia, and secondary sex characteristics. Despite the fact that bodies are biologically varied and complex, typically at birth the only assessment we get is a doctor or midwife—or, if your mom's timing was really off, cabdriver—looking between our legs and boldly assigning us a sex. Depending on the outward appearance of our genitals, these assignments can be either "It's a boy!" or "It's a girl!" or "I'm not quite sure." For some people that sex assignment fits (cisgender people) and for some it doesn't (transgender people and also some intersex people).

Here is a diagram showing biological sex as a continuum:

Female - - - - - - - - - - - - - - - - - - - Intersex - - - - - - - - - - - - - - - - - - - Male

Intersex individuals are folks whose chromosomes and/or biological sex characteristics (i.e., genitals, reproductive organs, and/or hormones) are not typical. (Please note the respectful use of the word *typical* rather than *normal*.) People who fall under the intersex umbrella have all sorts of natural variations and have existed throughout time. The old term *hermaphrodite*, which has a much narrower definition, is outdated, stigmatizes natural body variation, and should no longer be used. Please cross that word out in your head and replace it with *intersex*.

A few examples of people who fall under the intersex umbrella are:

- People who have genitalia that are not typical and the doctor or midwife is unable to assign a sex at birth.

- People who were assigned a sex at birth, later have fertility issues as adults, have genetic testing done, and find out that they have atypical chromosomes.
- People who were assigned female at birth, never menstruate, and find out as teenagers that instead of ovaries they have undescended testicles.

One of my favorite quotes about natural biological variation comes from Alice Dreger, professor of medical humanities and bioethics at Northwestern University: "There isn't really one simple way to sort out males and females. . . . And the science actually tells us sex is messy. Or as I like to say, humans like categories neat, but nature is a slob."[2]

Don't believe her? Think about the challenges the International Olympic Committee has been experiencing as it tries to sort athletes into "true" male and "true" female categories so they can compete. It can't be done. Physical examinations, chromosome testing, and hormone level assessments have all been put in place over the years in an attempt to fit athletes into two binary boxes of males and females, but many athletes still can't be categorized that way. Sex verification testing (which identifies sex chromosomes) and testosterone level testing have both proven to be inaccurate and discriminatory. Many athletes deemed "male imposters" were later found to be intersex.

I used to believe that being intersex was extremely rare—a common misunderstanding. What I have learned is that there is a large number of folks who fall under the intersex umbrella. The estimate is that intersex individuals make up about 1.7 percent of the population, making it as common as being a natural redhead.[3]

Why is the general perception that being intersex is extremely rare? One reason is that before we had the ability to do genetic testing, most of the people who were identified as intersex were only the ones who had atypical genitalia at birth. Another reason is because historically, there has been a lot of shame and secrecy around intersex individuals and their bodies.

Starting in the 1960s, doctors had the ability to perform cosmetic surgery on infants to "normalize" the appearance of their genitals. It quickly became common practice to perform surgery, almost immediately after birth, on babies who had genital variations, obviously without their consent. More often than not their genitalia were crafted to look like vaginas, because it was easier to surgically construct a vagina than a penis. (This is still true today.) The thinking back in the 1960s was that gender was completely dependent on socialization, not biology—nurture rather than nature. Therefore, the thought was, if you surgically craft a vagina on a two-day-old infant, dress the baby in pink, give the baby a girl's name, and purchase dolls for the baby, all will be well. But

HELPFUL HINT

The next time you see a parent with a newborn baby, instead of asking, "Is it a boy or a girl?" try, "What a beautiful baby! What's the baby's name?"

as it turns out, our gender identity, which we know at a very young age, is not influenced by the color of our clothes and the toys we are given as children.[4]

Although this practice of immediate, nonconsensual surgery still continues today in some places, most medical facilities have stopped cosmetic surgeries on intersex infants. Instead, they are investing time and energy toward educating and supporting the parents because it's incredibly difficult to raise an intersex child, whose gender identity is not yet known, in a binary world.

In the past ten years or so, I have, thankfully, started to see an increase in intersex visibility. Many of those 1960s babies who had surgery performed on their bodies are pretty pissed, and they are speaking out about what happened to them. Some of them were never even told that surgery had been performed on their bodies, and many of them now have bodies that don't match their gender identity. Their bravery in sharing their stories helps destigmatize the intersex communities and informs the search for smarter solutions for the future.

If you are interested in this topic, I would highly recommend the documentary film *Intersexion*, where intersex individuals share their stories, and the book *As Nature Made Him*, the true story of a boy who was forced to live life as a girl after a botched circumcision.[5]

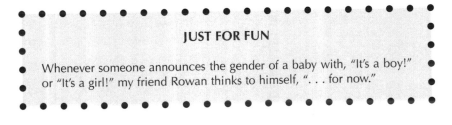

JUST FOR FUN

Whenever someone announces the gender of a baby with, "It's a boy!" or "It's a girl!" my friend Rowan thinks to himself, ". . . for now."

Gender Identity

The second component that makes up our sex, gender, and sexuality is gender identity. This is the answer to the question, "Are you a boy or girl?" or "Are you a man or woman?" The answer may be: "I'm a man," or "I'm a woman," or perhaps "Um . . . no." Many people believe that there are only two options when it comes to gender identity: You are a boy or a girl, a man or a woman. However,

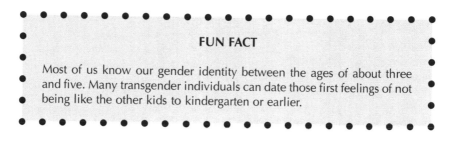

FUN FACT

Most of us know our gender identity between the ages of about three and five. Many transgender individuals can date those first feelings of not being like the other kids to kindergarten or earlier.

just like our beautiful array of varied bodies discussed in the previous section, there is also a beautiful array of gender identities.

Those of us who identify our gender as man or woman fit into the gender binary (i.e., relating to two things or two options). Folks who identify as nonbinary do not. Nonbinary individuals may identify themselves as having both genders, a different gender, several genders, or no gender at all. Some of the many identities that fall under the nonbinary umbrella are genderqueer, gender-fluid, agender, and Two-Spirit.

Note: If you're starting to get that overwhelmed feeling, please remember that you don't need to know or even necessarily understand all of the identities under the sun to be a good ally. Instead, let's have a thirty-second dance party

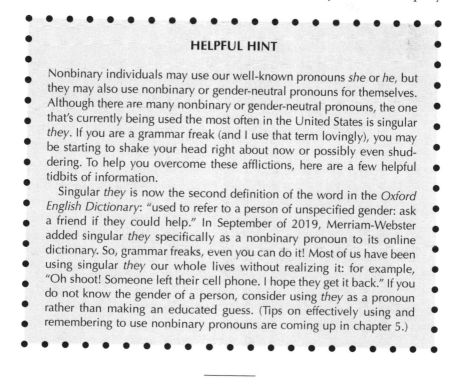

HELPFUL HINT

Nonbinary individuals may use our well-known pronouns *she* or *he*, but they may also use nonbinary or gender-neutral pronouns for themselves. Although there are many nonbinary or gender-neutral pronouns, the one that's currently being used the most often in the United States is singular *they*. If you are a grammar freak (and I use that term lovingly), you may be starting to shake your head right about now or possibly even shuddering. To help you overcome these afflictions, here are a few helpful tidbits of information.

Singular *they* is now the second definition of the word in the *Oxford English Dictionary*: "used to refer to a person of unspecified gender: ask a friend if they could help." In September of 2019, Merriam-Webster added singular *they* specifically as a nonbinary pronoun to its online dictionary. So, grammar freaks, even you can do it! Most of us have been using singular *they* our whole lives without realizing it: for example, "Oh shoot! Someone left their cell phone. I hope they get it back." If you do not know the gender of a person, consider using *they* as a pronoun rather than making an educated guess. (Tips on effectively using and remembering to use nonbinary pronouns are coming up in chapter 5.)

(Thank you, *Grey's Anatomy*!) and celebrate the diversity of all of the wonderful people on this planet.

Here is a diagram of the gender identity component:

Woman - - - - - - - - - - - - - - - - - - Nonbinary - - - - - - - - - - - - - - - - - - - Man

People will fall in different places all over this continuum. Visualize the billions of dots, please.

Gender Expression

For those of us who were identified as either male or female at birth and, as we grew, found that assignment matched our gender identity, we may be feeling all "ho-hum" right now. Well, hang on to your rainbow beanies! This third component gets pretty exciting for almost all of us.

Gender expression has to do with how we express our gender to the world. We do this with our clothing, hairstyles, activities, movements, and mannerisms. Some of this may be conscious choices we make for ourselves, like what we choose to wear and how we style our hair. These may also be unconscious things that we do or say that others pick up on, like the way we gesture or how much space we take up in a room. Society typically categorizes gender expression as being feminine, masculine, or androgynous (defined as neither feminine nor masculine, or as a blending of the two).

Feminine - - - - - - - - - - - - - - - Androgynous - - - - - - - - - - - - - - - Masculine

Our gender expression may change over time as we age. We may express our gender differently from day to day. We may even exhibit, at the same time, behaviors that are identified by our culture and society as feminine and ones that are identified as masculine. For example, picture a woman with long red nails under the hood of her car changing her oil.

You may have read that sentence about the woman changing her oil and experienced a bit of anger or frustration as you thought to yourself, "Well, who the hell gets to define what is masculine and feminine? Who gets to declare that changing the oil in your car is a masculine behavior?" I feel your anger and I second it! This stuff pisses me off no end. Who *does* get to decide this stuff? I have no idea. Similarly, I have wondered, in countries where nouns are all identified as either masculine or feminine (for example, a table in French is feminine), what do they do when there is a new thing? When the telephone was invented, was there a gender committee that got to decide whether it was masculine or feminine? This is such odd stuff.

An educated guess can help us figure out where some of the masculine and feminine labels came from. Because of biology, women traditionally took on the tasks of nurturing the babies, cooking, and tending the home. Men, unfettered by pregnancy and nursing, took on the hunting and the heavy labor. So it's easy to understand how these roles became gendered. But how, when, and why did we decide to gender things like musical instruments and colors?

Even though this irritates many of us, if I asked you to create a list of colors, behaviors, clothes, activities, and mannerisms that are considered feminine and masculine you could probably do it pretty easily. We all know this stuff and are pretty much inundated with it daily.

Also of note is the fact that lists of what's considered masculine versus feminine vary greatly depending on culture and society. What is considered masculine behavior in some cultures and societies may be considered feminine in other places of the world. Think about a man walking around with a satchel, considered a masculine behavior in London. Pick that guy up and plop him down in rural Mississippi and that look is going to be considered pretty feminine. In some countries, men walk around holding hands with other men; it's a sign of friendship. In other countries, two men holding hands are likely to be the target of nasty comments or even violence.

It's clear that this stuff is culturally and socially defined, not innate. And, in my humble opinion, it's pretty nonsensical—but holy smokes is it powerful! It has affected *all* of us, no matter how we identify. Most likely every single one of us was told at some point in our lives (or at many points), "Boys don't do that," or, "Girls don't do that." I remember many moments during my childhood where I was "guided" toward doing the more feminine thing. In third grade when we got to choose a musical instrument to play, I chose the drums; I was promptly told I had to choose something else because drums were a "boy instrument." I was told that the flute and the clarinet were good choices for girls. I did not yet know the word *badass*, or that I aspired to be one, so I complied. I played the clarinet (very poorly) for the required amount of time and then immediately quit. I could have been the next Ringo Starr, but I was restricted by gender norms!

The societal and cultural pressure to stay in our rigidly defined gendered boxes, known as gender policing, was very real when I was growing up and is still very real today. Every single one of us has been affected by it and all of our children are affected by it. Gender policing limits our creativity and our ability to live life as our authentic selves. It's at the heart of so much pain, fear, self-hatred, homophobia, biphobia, and transphobia.

Many homophobic/biphobic/transphobic actions and behaviors (e.g., name calling, bullying, and violence) are precipitated not by the target's sexual orientation or gender identity, but by their gender expression. It is gender policing taken to an extreme level. Think about an eight-year-old boy who plays the flute, who doesn't like sports, and whose favorite shirt is pink. That kid is likely being picked on at school, and he's probably being called "gay." That kid may not have a clue what his sexual orientation is yet. He is being picked on for not behaving "masculine" enough.

A few years ago, here in Upstate New York, two straight cisgender guy friends were sitting at a bar drinking beer. Two other guys in the bar picked up on something about these two friends and their gender expression and decided that they were a gay couple. When the two friends left the bar, they were jumped by the other guys, verbally abused with homophobic slurs, and severely beaten. These two straight, cisgender men were victims of homophobia-related violence based not on their sexual orientation, but on their gender expression.

So gender expression is the category where most of us have personal experience being somewhere along the continuum, rather than at one end or the other. It's likely that almost everyone expresses, at any given time, a blending of masculine and feminine mannerisms, hairstyles, clothing, activities, and movements. At this moment, as I write, I am sporting a feminine long hairstyle, a masculine sweatshirt, feminine leggings, and I am sitting with one leg up on my desk in an extremely "unladylike" manner. I'm blending!

Let's take a look at the first three components that we just reviewed:

Biological Sex

Female - - - - - - - - - - - - - - - - - - - Intersex - Male

Gender Identity

Woman - - - - - - - - - - - - - - - - - - Nonbinary - Man

Gender Expression

Feminine - - - - - - - - - - - - - - - - Androgynous - - - - - - - - - - - - - - - Masculine

Question: What do they all have in common?

Answer: They are all solely about us.

Now we are about to move into territory relating to others: attraction and intimate behaviors. These two components often get confused and conflated with the other three components, but they are completely separate parts of our identity.

Attraction (Also Known as Orientation)

Attraction has to do with who (if anyone) makes our hearts go pitter-patter. Sometimes this category is labeled *sexual orientation*, but I refer to it simply as "attraction" because not all orientations and attractions are sexual. Our attractions may be sexual or romantic (also known as *affectional*). Some people feel that romantic and affectional attraction are two distinct types of attractions, but most consider them to be the same. For the sake of clarity, I will refer to them as the same and will use them interchangeably in this book.

Generally, sexual attraction has to do with people we want to engage in sexual activities with (passionate kissing, sexual intercourse, oral sex, etc.). Romantic or affectional attraction has to do with people we want to engage in emotional and affectionate behaviors with (holding hands, snuggling, talking on the phone for hours, etc.). For those of you who are sexually and romantically attracted to the same types of people and you can't piece these types of attraction apart, you may now have a big, old question mark over your head, but it's important to know that for some folks these two types of attraction are distinctly different.

If you haven't already, you are likely to begin to hear people separate these different types of attractions. For example, a woman may describe herself as heterosexual and biromantic. For her this might mean that she wants to engage in sexual behaviors only with men, but she wants to engage in romantic/affectional behaviors with both men and women. A man may define himself as being asexual and heteroromantic. For him this might mean that he has no interest in engaging in sexual behaviors with anyone, but he wants to engage in romantic/affectional behaviors with women.

People may potentially be attracted to no one, to anyone, or to very specific types of people. Please note the use of the word *potentially* in this last sentence. I am straight. That doesn't mean that I am attracted to every man I see. I simply have the potential to be attracted to men.

Some of the many ways that people define their sexual attractions are gay, lesbian, bisexual, pansexual, asexual, and straight. Some of the many ways that people define their romantic attractions are homoromantic, biromantic, panromantic, aromantic, and heteroromantic.

Here is a diagram of the component of attraction or orientation.

Potentially Attracted to Men - - - - - - - - - - - - - - - - Potentially Attracted to Both/Anyone/No one - - - - - - - - - - - - - - - - Potentially Attracted to Women

POP QUIZ

What does *pansexual* mean?

A. The person is potentially sexually attracted to Disney characters.
B. The person is potentially sexually attracted to cookware.
C. The person is potentially sexually attracted to anyone, regardless of gender.

Answer: C

Pansexual typically means that the person has the potential to be attracted to anyone. I have heard people describe their pansexuality as being attracted to "hearts not parts." How does being pansexual differ from being bisexual? A fine question! It may not differ at all. Remember how identities mean different things to different people? Well two people with the same type of attraction may use different identity words to define that for themselves. So why did we need another term when we already had the term *bisexual*? For some folks the word *bisexual* was too binary. Although the definition is changing, the term *bisexual* originally implied that a person was attracted to only men and women. What if the person is attracted to nonbinary people who don't identify as men or women? The word *pansexual* gets away from that binary thinking. Now, I have met many people who use the word *bisexual* but they define it this way: "I'm attracted to people who are like me and my gender and to people who are a different gender." That's how the *bi*—the two options—gets defined for them. The moral of the story, once again, is to listen to how people identify and use those terms.

Intimate Behaviors

Intimate behaviors are what we actually do. These may be sexual behaviors or they may be romantic behaviors. Here is the final component for our model.

With	With	With
Men -	Both/Anyone/ - - - - - - - - - - - - - - - - - -	Women
	No one	

We might think that what we do sexually and romantically will always line up with our attractions, but this is not always the case. These two components, at-

POP QUIZ

You see two teenage girls kissing in the school parking lot. How do they identify?

A. They are lesbians.
B. They are straight. They are just kissing because their boyfriends think it's hot.
C. They are bisexual or pansexual.
D. They are questioning.
E. We have absolutely no idea.

Answer: E

I'm feeling confident that you knew the answer to this one. Simply seeing a behavior tells us nothing about how someone identifies, what their motivation is, or whom they are attracted to.

traction and intimate behaviors, may not align for many different reasons. One possible reason is societal pressures: for example, the teenage boy who knows that he is gay (his attraction) but is sleeping with as many girls as he can (his behaviors) in an attempt to prove to others that he is straight. Another reason why these components might not align is that we do not necessarily act on all of our attractions at once. For example, a pansexual married woman who is only having sexual behaviors with her husband has not suddenly become straight. Her attraction or sexual orientation has not changed; she is still pansexual.

The confusion over attractions and behaviors is at the heart of many of the misunderstandings about LGBTQ+ people. As I mentioned in chapter 3, when people hear anything having to do with LGBTQ+ identities, their heads often go right to sexual behaviors. It's at the core of the comment, "I don't mind gay people; I just wish they would keep it in the bedroom." It's also, I believe, one of the main reasons why essential education around LGBTQ+ identities and inclusion is not currently being adequately offered in United States K–12 schools. Parents and teachers are afraid that the conversation will be about sexual behaviors.

Take a look at the entire model with all five components.

Biological Sex

Female -Intersex - Male

Gender Identity

Woman - - - - - - - - - - - - - - - - - Nonbinary - - - - - - - - - - - - - - - - - - - Man

Gender Expression

Feminine - - - - - - - - - - - - - - - Androgynous - - - - - - - - - - - - - - - - Masculine

Attraction

Potentially	Potentially	Potentially
Attracted	Attracted to	Attracted
to Men - - - - - - - - - - - - - - - Both/Anyone/ - - - - - - - - - - - - - - - to Women		
	No one	

Intimate Behaviors

With	With	With
Men - - - - - - - - - - - - - - - - - Both/Anyone/ - - - - - - - - - - - - - - - - Women		
	No one	

The first four components (biological sex, gender identity, gender expression, and attraction) come with us everywhere and are a part of who we are. They come to work, school, the grocery store, etc. Intimate behaviors is the only component that should not be brought into the workplace or school.

In order to help people understand the differences between attraction and intimate behaviors, I like to offer very concrete examples like this one. Let's say I'm a schoolteacher and my students ask me, "Hey, Ms. Gainsburg, what did you do over the weekend?" and I answer, "My husband and I discovered this great new sexual position." This is an example of being out with my intimate behaviors. Not okay. But the response, "My wife and I saw this great movie" is an example of being out about my relationship status, related to my attraction or my orientation, which is just peachy.

The distinction between attractions and behaviors is also extremely important for those who work in a healthcare setting. It's imperative that those in healthcare ask the right questions in order to get the answers they need to take care of people. So, when doing screenings for sexually transmitted infections, questions should be about a person's sexual behaviors, *not* about how they identify their orientation. Too often healthcare workers either ignore these questions altogether (assuming that everyone is straight) or ask about a patient's orientation (e.g., "Do you identify as LGBT?"). The term *MSM*, which stands for "men who have sex with men" and is often used in communities of color, was created for this exact reason. Men who identified as straight but were having sex with

POP QUIZ

Picture someone you have never met walking down the street. There is only one component that we see or "know" about someone. Which one is it?

A. Biological sex
B. Gender identity
C. Gender expression
D. Attraction
E. Intimate behaviors

Answer: C

Gender expression is the only component we see or "know" about people. We do not see the person's genitals, chromosomes, or hormone levels. We don't know how they identify their gender unless they tell us. We don't know their orientation or whom they are attracted to. And if they are just walking down the street, we are not seeing their intimate behaviors. All we see and pick up on is the person's gender expression. We see their hair, clothes, jewelry, whether or not they have tattoos, and the way they move, and very often we *think* we can fill in the other components. We make assumptions about people's biological sex, their gender identity, whom they are attracted to, and, let's face it, probably also what they are doing in the bedroom, based solely on their gender expression. For example: We may see a woman in high heels, makeup, a dress, and long hair (gender expression) and we may assume that she has a vagina and ovaries (biological sex), identifies as a women (gender identity), is attracted only to men (attraction), and is sexually and romantically active only with men (intimate behaviors). Sometimes we're right, but lots of times we're wrong—and, unless we're the person's lover or doctor, typically we will never know.

The way that humans make sense of the world is by putting things and people into categories. It's something we do naturally. In this case, try to fight it. Whenever you find yourself thinking, "I bet that guy is gay," or, "I think she may be trans," give yourself an imaginary dope slap.

other men were not getting the care they needed at health centers because the centers were not identifying their sexual behaviors. Healthcare providers should think about what information they need to treat the whole person and use this information to craft their intake forms.

Understanding the differences between attractions and behaviors and being able to explain these differences to others is a critical role that a savvy ally can play as we create a better and more inclusive world.

WHERE DO I FALL?

And now, for your reading pleasure, and as promised, I will map myself out using this basic diagram of the components of sex, gender, and sexuality. I'll admit, the first time this model was shown to me I thought to myself, "This is going to be so boring for me. I am so plain vanilla. I'll be all on one side." However, it was actually a pretty eye-opening experience.

Biological Sex

I have never had genetic testing, but I was able to reproduce and create two wonderful children, so I am going to guess and put myself around here:

Female - - - - - - - - - - - - - - - - - - Intersex - Male

ME

Gender Identity

I have never questioned my gender identity. The doctor said, "It's a girl!" and that always fit for me. So I am going to put myself here.

Woman - - - - - - - - - - - - - - - - - - Nonbinary - - - - - - - - - - - - - - - - - - - Man

ME

Gender Expression

Here is where things got more interesting for me. I have spent a great deal of my life looking at women who, in our society and culture, would be considered very feminine (e.g., high heels, lacey underthings, and makeup) and thinking to myself: "I feel as far from that as I do from being a dude, but I know I am a woman. What the heck?" Until I saw this diagram I didn't have the language to make sense of this. When this diagram was drawn out for me by a friend on a napkin in a coffeehouse, I definitely had one of those lightbulb moments. I am a woman and I have always known that. It's my gender expression that has had me confused.

When I think honestly about mapping myself out on the continuum of gender expression, I realize that my gender expression is all over the place and that it varies depending on the situation and on my surroundings. For example, I tend to express more femininity when I dress formally to facilitate a workshop or go out to dinner, but when found in my natural habitat, my gender expression is much more masculine. Therefore, I map myself like this:

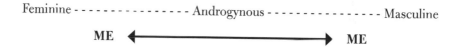

Attraction

When I first saw this model, the only orientation I was aware of was sexual orientation, and I placed myself solidly in the "attracted to men" section. Since that time, my understanding of attraction has grown. As I began to learn about affectional attraction, I suddenly remembered some crushes I had on girls and women. These crushes confused me at the time because I knew I did not want to have sex with these women. However, I looked up to them, was incredibly flattered by their attention, and, if I'm honest with myself, wouldn't have minded some PG-rated hand-holding or snuggling with them. So, I map myself like this:

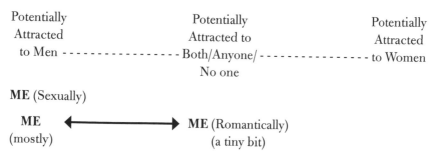

Note: I am currently running into a *major* design flaw with this model, which is why sexuality and gender educator Sam Killermann developed the "-Ness" model. (More on this coming soon.)

Intimate Behaviors

Okay, here we go. I know you are all dying to know what straight people actually do in the bedroom. Well . . . although I sometimes get a hamstring cramp, one of my favorite sexual positions is where I take my right leg and . . . oh, wait—this is the one I'm *not* supposed to share, right? (Just making sure you're paying attention.) Let me just say that my intimate behaviors have all been with men.

With Men	With Both/Anyone/ No one	With Women

ME (Sexually)
ME (Romantically)

AN ADVANCED DIAGRAM OF THE COMPONENTS OF SEX, GENDER, AND SEXUALITY

I mentioned previously that I ran into a major design flaw as I was mapping myself out. The main reason I shared the basic diagram is that it's fairly simple. If you, as an ally, are helping other folks understand the different components that make up our sex, gender, and sexuality and it's the first time this information has been presented to them, it's a really good diagram to use. However, it definitely has some flaws.

One flaw with this basic diagram is that it sets up a linear continuum, with "female/woman/feminine/attracted to men/with men" on one side and "male/man/masculine/attracted to women/with women" on the other. The implication is that anything other than these two sides is "the middle." Why is that a problem? Well, for one thing, it makes the two ends seem like the norm, with all of that "unusual" stuff in the middle.

Another weakness with this basic diagram is that things in the middle can be really different from other things in the middle, but there is no way to demonstrate that. For example: both asexual (usually defined as having no sexual attraction) and pansexual (usually defined as potentially being attracted to anyone) are in the middle in this basic diagram, but they are *very* different orientations.

Killermann has created an advanced diagram that he calls the "-Ness" model.[6] In this model, the components are mapped out on a sliding scale. Although his diagram is not perfect, it solves the problems associated with "the middle" because there *is* no middle. For example, under the component of attraction, a person can map out how much they are attracted to women and how much they are attracted to men using arrows of different lengths. Therefore, our asexual friend and our pansexual friend can map themselves very differently using this advanced diagram.

An asexual person might map themselves like this:

Sexually attracted to . . .

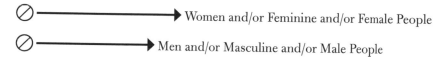

And our pansexual friend might map themselves like this:

Sexually attracted to . . .

⊘ ——————————————→ Women and/or Feminine and/or Female People

⊘ ——————————→ Men and/or Masculine and/or Male People

The "-Ness" model also gets away from the idea that the two sides are opposites, which is how it appears in the basic diagram. Male and female, man and woman, masculine and feminine are not opposites. As Killermann says, "Being more of one thing needn't require you to be less of another."[7] If I am hunting (an activity we tend to think of in our society as masculine), it does not make me less feminine. In the basic model, moving more toward the masculine side pulls you away from the feminine side. In the "-Ness" model the levels for each can be represented independently, like this:

Gender Expression

Another flaw with the basic diagram that I ran into while mapping myself out is that it doesn't distinguish between the different types of attractions or orientations. Killermann's "-Ness" model has two attraction scales, one for sexual attraction and one for romantic (or affectional) attraction. So a gay man who is biromantic could make that distinction like this:

Sexually attracted to . . .

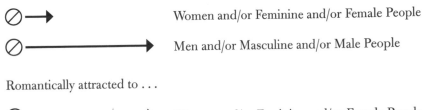

Women and/or Feminine and/or Female People

Men and/or Masculine and/or Male People

Romantically attracted to . . .

Women and/or Feminine and/or Female People

Men and/or Masculine and/or Male People

As allies, we should think about which diagram will help someone with their understanding of sex, gender, and sexuality the most. In general, I find that the basic diagram is best for folks who have never thought much about this topic, while the advanced model is better for higher-level, more nuanced conversations. If you are jazzed by this topic and want to know even more about sexuality and especially gender, I would strongly encourage you to pick up Sam Killermann's book *A Guide to Gender: The Social Justice Advocate's Handbook*. It's a super informative and extremely fun read.

ANSWERS TO OUR QUESTIONS

Now that we have reviewed the different components that make up our sex, gender, and sexuality, let's go back to the four questions from the beginning of this chapter and get some answers.

What the Heck Does *Nonbinary* Mean?

Nonbinary describes people who do not fit into the two typical binary gendered options, man or woman. People who identify as nonbinary may describe themselves as having no gender, having a different gender from man or woman, having both genders, having multiple genders, and more. Nonbinary folks may use gender-neutral or genderless pronouns like singular *they*.

Can Transgender People Also Be Gay?

Absolutely. *Transgender* has to do with gender and *gay* has to do with attraction or orientation. They are completely separate things. A transgender person can be gay, straight, lesbian, pansexual, asexual, or bisexual, just as cisgender people can be any of those things.

Now when you see *LGBT* you know these identities are orientation-orientation-orientation-gender. The *Q* or *Queer* can be either an orientation or a gender, or both (see table 4.1).

The idea of a gay transgender man or a lesbian transgender woman can really confuse people. I have often been asked, "If a trans man was assigned female at birth and is attracted to men, why the heck didn't he just stay a woman?" The thinking behind this, I believe, is that this man fit into our gendered boxes much better as a straight woman than he does as a gay trans man. Why would he put himself through all the trouble of transitioning and then living a potentially difficult life as a gay trans guy in a homophobic and transphobic world? The answer is that living a life where you cannot be your authentic self *is* a difficult life, and it's incredibly painful. We cannot simply choose our gender or orientation because it makes life easier. A gay trans man knows himself to be a man and he would like to be intimate with men as a man. Although what I am about to write confuses orientation with behavior, I am going to say it anyway because many people have found this helpful: *Very* simply put, one is who we sleep with (orientation) and one is who we sleep as (gender identity).

How Can I Tell If Someone Is Gay?

This one is easy. You can't. All you can see is someone's gender expression. The management is not responsible for any conjectures made by the reader. Assume at your own risk.

How Can Someone Identify as Asexual but Still Have Sex?

An asexual person has little or no interest in sexual behaviors. That tells us nothing about what they are actually doing sexually. They may be in a relationship with someone who enjoys sex and they may choose to engage in those behaviors for their partner. Not having sex is celibacy (behavior); not having sexual attraction is asexuality (orientation).

Table 4.1. Terms and Identity Types

Identity Term	Lesbian	Gay	Bisexual	Transgender	Queer
Type of Identity	Orientation	Orientation	Orientation	Gender	Either/Both

KEY ALLY TAKEAWAYS

- We are curious beings, but assumptions are dangerous. All we typically see or "know" about people is their gender expression. Do not attempt to fill in the rest (i.e., biological sex, gender identity, attraction, and intimate behaviors). As allies, we should focus on what we need to know about a person—often, simply how someone would like to be addressed or referred to—in order to be respectful.
- Being out in the workplace or at school means living authentically and not having to lie or be deceptive. It doesn't mean talking about sexual behaviors. It's not a "bedroom issue." People are LGBTQ+ 24/7.
- Without gender policing, we would all live much freer and more authentic lives.

NOTES

1. The basic diagram used in this chapter is based on Michael G. Shively and John P. DeCecco, "Components of Sexual Identity," *Journal of Homosexuality* 3, no. 1 (1977): 41–48, https://www.tandfonline.com/doi/abs/10.1300/J082v03n01_04.

2. Christopher Clarey, "Gender Test after a Gold-Medal Finish," *New York Times*, August 19, 2009, https://www.nytimes.com/2009/08/20/sports/20runner.html.

3. Hida, "How Common Is Intersex? An Explanation of the Stats," Intersex Campaign for Equality, April 1, 2015, https://www.intersexequality.com/how-common-is-intersex-in-humans/.

4. Jason Rafferty, "Gender Development in Children," American Academy of Pediatrics, September 18, 2018, https://www.healthychildren.org/English/ages-stages/grade school/Pages/Gender-Identity-and-Gender-Confusion-In-Children.aspx.

5. John Keir (producer) and Lahood Grant (director), *Intersexion: Gender Ambiguity Unveiled* (Kilbirnie, Wellington, New Zealand: Ponsonby Production Limited, 2012), DVD. John Colapinto, *As Nature Made Him: The Boy Who Was Raised as a Girl* (New York: HarperCollins, 2000).

6. Sam Killermann, *A Guide to Gender: The Social Justice Advocate's Handbook*, rev. and updated ed. (Austin, TX: Impetus Books, 2017), ch. 13.

7. Ibid., 249.

Part II

BUILDING SKILLS FOR HAVING RESPECTFUL CONVERSATIONS

LGBTQ+ ETIQUETTE

Be excellent to each other!

—Bill S. Preston, Esq. (from *Bill
and Ted's Excellent Adventure*)

Now here's the good stuff! This chapter offers the actionable language that will allow you to respectfully navigate conversations with LGBTQ+ people even if you forget all of the words in the glossary or don't know all of the identities under the LGBTQ+ umbrella. These are six best-practice tips for having respectful conversations with LGBTQ+ people (or anyone, for that matter)."[1] If you've already got these down, then take them out into the world. These are great pointers for savvy allies to share with others to help create more respectful environments for everyone.

TIP #1: MIRROR TERMS

I'm starting with what is one of my favorite tips and the most important way to show respect to all people with our language, not just people in the LGBTQ+ communities: Listen carefully and mirror the terms that people use for themselves. It's so beautifully simple and will take you so far.

Imagine someone says to me, "As a *queer* woman, I find it difficult when people make faulty assumptions and assume that I am straight." If I respond with, "I know I am guilty of making those errors myself. Since you are a *lesbian*, I would love to hear what suggestions you have for me so that I can change my language," then I have just demonstrated to this woman that I am not listening. I am making assumptions and labeling someone according to my glossary of terms. Ugh! Didn't I warn myself to use that darn glossary with caution? Most likely I thought to myself, "This is clearly a woman who likes other women; therefore, she must be a lesbian. I will use that term." However, this individual used the word *queer* to identify herself. I should have listened and mirrored that term.

The mirroring of terms is also important when people are talking about their loved ones and family members. If I invite a friend from work to my house for a party and as he walks in, he says, "This is my *husband*, Javier," and I respond with, "Hey everyone! This is Marc's *partner*, Javier," then once again, I am not listening or using my respectful communication tip. I should have mirrored Marc's language and introduced Javier as his husband.

One final point to note here is that if we have a most excellent conversation with someone and use their terms and identities, we should not assume that the

---

POP QUIZ

Who does the queer woman in the above scenario have sex with? Does she have sex only with women? Does she have sex with men and women? Does she have sex with people regardless of their gender? Does she have sex at all? Choose all that apply:

A. She has sex only with women; otherwise she would have said she was bisexual or pansexual.
B. We have no way of knowing unless we ask.
C. It's none of our business.

Answer: Both B and C

We have no way of knowing unless we ask (and let's not ask unless we know her really, really well) and it's none of our business (unless we are her doctor). All we know from what she has told us above is that she doesn't identify as straight. We don't know whom she is attracted to, whom she has sex with, or even if she has sex at all. We just know she identifies as queer, and that's all we need to know to have respectful conversations with her and about her.

---

next person we talk to uses the same terms. In other words, now that I know the woman in the first scenario uses the word *queer* to identify herself, the next time I meet two women who are together as a couple, I should not refer to them as queer. But how *should* I refer to these two women if I don't know how they identify? I would avoid using an identity term altogether. I would simply say something like, "I met a great couple at your party last week. What were those women's names again?"

TIP #2: UNGENDER LANGUAGE

In workshops, when I recommend that people ungender their language, invariably someone will make a comment like this: "I asked the gentleman about his wife and he just corrected me and let me know that he had a husband. It was no big deal."

It may have been no big deal for the asker, but we have no idea whether it was a big deal for this married man. What went through *his* head before he shared that he was actually married to a man? Annoyance? Discomfort? Anxiety? Was he concerned for his safety? Did he look around to see who else was listening? It *is* possible that it was no big deal for this man, but it's a pretty big deal for many.

One of my workshop participants who pushed back on this tip was an elementary school teacher. I tried the "switch it" technique with her, changing the scenario to a school setting with young children. I asked her to think about saying "Merry Christmas" to her class as they left for winter break, rather than "Happy Holidays." I told her that she may have a student who feels comfortable raising their hand and saying, "My family celebrates Hanukkah." However, she may also have a student who is thinking, "Does my teacher think that everyone celebrates Christmas? Perhaps Hanukkah isn't as important or as valued as Christmas. Maybe my teacher doesn't like Jewish people. I had better not let on that I celebrate Hanukkah."

Sometimes the "switch it" technique works extremely well and lightbulbs go off. Unfortunately, in this case the lightbulb did not go off. This teacher told me that she still says, "Merry Christmas" to her class because that's what most of her students celebrate. Bummer. (See chapter 7 for a discussion on planting seeds and how people learn.)

Back to our ungendering language tip: If you're not wearing a big rainbow button on your shirt that says "I'm an ally!" (which I highly recommend, by the way), this is the next best way you can indicate to an LGBTQ+ person that you are aware that LGBTQ+ people are out there among us and that you support them. Seriously, LGBTQ+ people and their loved ones are looking and listening.

A few months ago, I was sitting next to a woman on a plane when we got into a conversation about where we each were going.

"I am continuing on to Denver. My daughter is getting married," she said.

And I said, "Oh wow! Congratulations! Are you pleased with her choice in a partner?"

The woman hesitated for a moment and then said, "Yes. I am. And I'm really pleased that you used the word 'partner.' She is marrying a woman."

If I had asked, "Are you pleased with her choice in a husband?" she might have corrected me or she might have simply said, "Mm-hmm" and turned back to read her emergency landing card in the seat back pocket. The point is that by using the word *partner*, I told her with my language that I was open to hearing her tell me that her daughter was marrying anyone under the sun.

The assumption that everyone is straight (also known as *heteronormativity*) is extremely common and not necessarily meant to be hurtful—and we are all guilty of it, myself included. Remember my friend Jonathan from chapter 3, the gay man who was buying flowers for his husband at the grocery store? Let's look closer at what happened when that cashier said, "Oh, those are beautiful. Are they for your wife?"

If Jonathan had been purchasing the flowers for his wife, he might have simply said, "Yes," and moved on, completely unaware that this question could cause stress or fear for anyone. But Jonathan was purchasing the flowers for his husband, so he was now backed into a corner by the cashier's language. He had three options:

Lie: "Yes. They are for my wife."
Deflect: "I think you just dropped my tomato."
Come out: "No, actually they're for my husband."

For many LGBTQ+ people, this is an anxiety-filled moment. What if they are out to their friends, but not to their parents? Should they be telling the grocery store cashier their orientation when their parents don't even know? What if an incredibly homophobic person is standing in line behind them, listening in? Might that person harass them or even become violent in the parking lot?

By using ungendered language we avoid putting people on the spot, we create safer environments, and we let people know that we are aware that straight and cisgender are not the only ways to be.

POP QUIZ

What would have been a better way for this cashier to have made small talk with Jonathan?

A. "Oh, those are beautiful flowers. Are they for your wife or husband?"
B. "Oh, those are beautiful flowers. Are they for your partner?"
C. "Oh, those are beautiful flowers. You're going to make someone's day with those."

Answer: C

Answer A is more inclusive, but it still puts Jonathan on the spot. Also, the language implies that everyone is binary and that everyone identifies as a man or a woman. As we discussed in chapter 4, not everyone does. Answer B is better than A but could potentially still cause anxiety by putting the person on the spot. Answer C is best. If the customer wants to have a conversation about who the flowers are for, they can. However, it also gives them an out to not identify in public. They can simply smile and say, "Yup."

Great words to remove from your vocabulary if you don't have any idea how someone identifies or likes to be addressed include *husband, wife, girlfriend, boyfriend, ladies, gentlemen, guys, Mr., Mrs., Miss, Sir,* and *Ma'am.*

Great words to add to your vocabulary if you don't have any idea how someone identifies or likes to be addressed are *partner* or *partners* (let's be mindful of our polyamorous friends), *loved one* or *loved ones, special person* or *people, significant other* or *others, important person* or *people, folks, team, friends,* and *y'all* (if you can pull it off).

COMBINING TIP #1 AND TIP #2

Now let's put what we learned in Tip #1 (mirror terms) together with what we learned in Tip #2 (ungender language). You may be wondering why the use of *partner* was okay for me to use on the airplane, but not okay in the previous example of Marc and Javier. *Partner* or *partners* are great ungendered terms to use if you don't know the gender of someone's loved one or loved ones. But once you receive information about how someone refers to their loved one it is respectful to mirror that term. Here's a best-practice step-by-step guide:

> *Step 1:* Throw ungendered words out into the universe when having conversations.
>
> Example: "Please feel free to bring your partner or partners to my party."
>
> *Step 2:* Listen to how people respond.
>
> Example: "Oh, well thank you very much. I would love to bring my wife to your party."
>
> *Step 3:* Mirror terms that people use to identify themselves and their loved ones.
>
> Example: "Wonderful! I am looking forward to meeting your wife."

TIP #3: CREATE SYSTEMS THAT WORK FOR EVERYONE

Too often I find that efforts toward being more inclusive involve the "tack it on" method, for example:

> Thank you for registering for our conference. We would like to make sure that this experience is as welcoming and inclusive as possible. Please check all that are applicable.
>
> ___ I need ASL interpretation
>
> ___ I would like a vegetarian lunch

This system involves identifying a need ("Hey! We should offer a vegetarian meal.") and tacking on a new option. But what about folks who are in wheelchairs? What about folks who have peanut allergies? Do we keep tacking on boxes as the needs occur to us, or do we create a system that works for everyone? Here is an example of a system that works for everyone:

> Thank you for registering for our conference. We would like to make sure that this experience is as welcoming and inclusive as possible. Please let us know if you have any dietary restrictions or accessibility needs below.
>
> ___ I do have dietary restrictions and/or accessibility needs. Please contact me.

The "tack it on" method also happens in conversations. We typically move through the world making assumptions about other people's gender. Often, we don't even think about these assumptions until we are faced with someone whose gender is unclear to us. Then, if we have not created systems that work for everyone, we find ourselves in awkward "tack it on" situations where we elbow the person next to us and whisper, "Is that a guy or a gal?"

In a situation where we are not sure of someone's gender, a good place to start is to ask ourselves, "Do I need to know this person's gender?" and, "Is this person's gender important for the conversation?" Many times the answer is no; we can often easily navigate conversations without knowing someone's gender.

Let's say a new client named Lee shows up for a counseling appointment. When speaking directly with Lee, the staff can navigate the conversation well without knowing how to refer to them. (Please note the use of the most excellent and versatile pronoun singular *they/them* used just now.) The staff would use the word *you* and *your* throughout the conversation, because they would be speaking directly to Lee. For example: "Did you bring your insurance card with you today?" Hurray for ungendered terms!

However, there are times when we actually do need to know how people refer to themselves in order to be respectful. When we talk *about* Lee, we have no idea which pronoun to use. For example, a staff member who says, "I'm just copying his insurance card" has most likely made a pronoun choice based on Lee's attire, hair length, hairstyle, and voice. They may also have taken a peek at the gender marker on Lee's insurance card and thought that this was a sure way of knowing Lee's gender. (*Hint:* It's not.) Based on all this information, the office staff member may have guessed correctly—or they may have just screwed up royally and bummed Lee out for the entire day. Using a gender-neutral pronoun would be a better choice in this situation, for example: "I'm just copying their insurance card."

The gender-neutral pronoun *they* is a good choice when faced with situations where we don't know someone's gender. An even better choice is to implement systems where we ask *everyone* how we can be respectful in our language when we refer to them. Handing every single client at this counseling center an intake form with an optional section that asks, "How may we respectfully refer to you?" and, "What pronouns do you use?" is not only a great way to prevent misgendering people but also a very welcoming indicator that the center is LGBTQ+ aware and supportive.

Sometimes clients may not be sure what you are asking, so it may be helpful to offer a few examples, like this:

"How may we respectfully refer to you?" (For example: *Mrs. Smith, Dr. Jones, Tom*)

"What pronouns do you use?" (For example: *he, she, they*)

If a client doesn't want to share this information, that's okay. Let them know that it's a standard question you ask all your clients and that it's optional. If you want, you can use your savvy ally skills to explain that the questions are included on the form in order to create the most inclusive space possible.

I am cisgender and I have the privilege of moving through the world and having people pretty much always guess correctly when they assume my gender. But I hate being called *Ma'am* or *Mrs. Gainsburg*. I can't even imagine how hurtful it would be if I were also being misgendered with these terms. In other words, it would be so much worse if I was being referred to as *Ma'am* or *Mrs. Gainsburg* and I was actually a man. I would love for all professional offices to have a form that allows me to choose how the staff refers to me. These questions on forms are great for learning how to respectfully address *everyone*.

How might this interaction play out in a situation where using a form isn't feasible? Let's look at a situation with a police officer pulling someone over. Police officers are typically trained to say *Sir* and *Ma'am*, as in, "Good evening, Ma'am. Do you know why I pulled you over and am about to hit you with a big, fat ticket?" Now, I know that there are people who like to be referred to as *Sir, Ma'am, Mr.,* or *Mrs.* For many folks, this is a sign of respect. So how do we navigate a world where some people want others to refer to them with formal gendered language and others will be made super happy by ungendered terms? Once again, whenever possible, we ask—and we ask *everyone*, not just the folks we look at and are not quite sure.

Here is what a more inclusive interaction might look like with this police officer and me:

> Police officer: Good evening. How may I address you tonight?
>
> Jeannie: You can call me Jeannie.
>
> Police officer: Do you know why I pulled you over and am about to hit you with a big, fat ticket, Jeannie?

Voilà!

TIP #4: USE THE CORRECT NAME AND PRONOUN

This one probably seems fairly obvious: Refer to people the way they want to be referred to. If you meet a new coworker whose name badge says William but they introduce themselves as Bill, you're probably going to use the name Bill. Easy-peasy. Now let's move on to a few situations that might be a bit more confusing.

Imagine you are supervising a transgender employee whose legal name is Jamal but who would like you to refer to them as Jasmine. What should you do? First of all, refer to them as Jasmine. Next you should ask, if you haven't already, "Which pronouns should I use for you?" It might make the situation more comfortable if you first share the pronouns you use for yourself: for example, "I use *she, her*, and *hers* as my pronouns. How may I refer to you?" Additionally, in a situation like this one, you should probably have a private conversation with Jasmine about how best to share Jasmine's name and pronouns with the other employees. A final best-practice tip is to keep Jasmine's legal name as confidential as possible, on a need-to-know basis only.

I have worked with many transgender coworkers. Some had legally changed their names and some had not. It did not matter to me as a coworker. I used their current name. I never asked what their name used to be or, even worse, what their "real" name was. (*Hint:* This is rude. See chapter 8 for more on common bloopers.)

You might work at an agency or company that has a policy demanding legal names be represented on all name badges, ID cards, and e-mail addresses. It stinks, but it's a reality in some workplaces. If this is the case where you work, here are some recommended ally actions:

- Work with your employee, or encourage the agency's leadership to work with the employee, to come up with creative "duct tape patch-up job" solutions that will help to make sure the employee is addressed properly. For example: Add a ribbon to the bottom of the employee's name badge that says, "Please call me Bill," or, "Please call me Jasmine."
- Normalize the "Please call me _____" ribbon by adding one to your own name badge and encouraging others to do the same. This way transgender employees are not easily identified and do not stand out as obviously different.
- Look at long-term "big fix" solutions that can make your workplace more inclusive in the future. Talk to your leadership or administrative team about the current policy and let them know it's problematic for some employees. Ask if there are adjustments that can be made to the legal name policies and the current confidentiality policies (i.e., policies put in place to protect employees' personal information). Be an advocate for change. (Read more about duct tape patch-up jobs and big fixes in chapter 10.)

We should also use a person's correct current name and pronouns when we are referring to their past. We should not do that thing in our heads where we

POP QUIZ

What is the correct and respectful way to talk about the Olympic gold medal–winning decathlete who won the medal before she transitioned?

A. Bruce Jenner won an Olympic gold medal.
B. Caitlyn Jenner won an Olympic gold medal, back when she was Bruce.
C. Caitlyn Jenner won an Olympic gold medal.

Answer: C

Even though we know that Caitlyn referred to herself using a different name and pronoun when she won the Olympics, it's correct and respectful to stay in the present with her name and identity, even when discussing the past.

think: "Hmmm. When my coworker Alice was five, she was a guy, so to be accurate I should switch back to Alfred and use the pronoun *he* when I talk about her as a young person." That is not cool, not respectful, and may be a safety issue for Alice.

If we say loudly in the cafeteria, "Hey Alice, when you were Alfred, did you play on any sports teams?" we have just outed Alice to everyone within hearing distance, potentially putting her at risk. We have probably also violated our company's confidentiality policies. The unfortunate reality is that we live in a very homophobic, biphobic, and transphobic world. In the LGBTQ+ communities, transgender women run the highest risk of being victims of violence. Transgender women of color are at the highest risk of all.[2] Your little slipup could have devastating consequences. Accuracy isn't a good enough excuse for being disrespectful with our language or for potentially putting someone's safety at risk.

I have often heard the comment, "This would be so much easier if they just legally changed their name!" I will not go into lengthy detail here describing the daunting, time-consuming, expensive, and sometimes humiliating process that trans folks have to go through to legally change their names. I will simply share a few eye-opening facts:

- In many states legal name changes and the person's current address must be published repeatedly in a newspaper for all to see. Many people are afraid to make their transition and their home address this public.

- In many states a person must petition the court for a legal name change. A judge may reject applications for transgender people, and many judges do.
- Separate name change applications must be submitted for Social Security, driver's license, birth certificate, passport, and more. Each department has different requirements. The total cost is typically hundreds of dollars, a financial burden that can be inhibiting for many people.

There may be other, more personal reasons why someone may decide not to legally change their name. I know a woman who felt unsafe sharing her identity at work. She was safe to be her authentic self only when she was at home or with friends. This unhappy situation doesn't make her any less trans than someone who has the support at work and the finances to be able to legally change their name. As allies we should always work hard to use a person's correct chosen name, regardless of whether it has been legally changed or not.

One final point to keep in mind is that how someone identifies (gender identity) and how they dress or wear their hair (gender expression) are completely different things. We don't ever want to think to ourselves, "Huh. Jasmine is wearing a tie today. I should probably use her old name, Jamal." Just because Jasmine is choosing to dress in a way that our society considers masculine doesn't mean that her gender identity has changed. People express themselves in all different ways. It doesn't change who they are.

TIP #5: ALLOW YOURSELF TO BE RAGGEDY

Early on in my work as an ally someone said to me, "Allow yourself to be raggedy." I absolutely love this. I find that in general, I am very quick to forgive others, but I am extremely hard on myself when I make a mistake. We need to give ourselves permission to be vulnerable, not know all of the answers, and mess up sometimes.

Part of the process of allowing ourselves to be raggedy involves speaking from the heart. Examples of speaking from the heart to start a conversation include: "I mean to be respectful; please forgive me if I mess up initially," or, "A lot of this is new to me. Please feel free to correct me if I use the wrong term." These conversation starters make it clear that we are ready and willing to learn.

What should an apology look like if you do make a mistake? In general, it should be similar to accidentally bumping into someone. If you bump into someone on the street you are unlikely to walk by without saying anything, but you are also unlikely to get down on your knees, tell the person how awful you feel, and beg for their forgiveness. You will probably simply say something like, "Oh, excuse me," and move on.

If you're reading this book, my guess is you are a person who is interested in being as respectful as possible, so it's likely that when you mess up you are going to feel terrible and your instinct might be to over-apologize. In general, this makes the situation worse because you have shifted the focus onto yourself. The person who you messed up with now may feel the need to make *you* feel better. So try not to draw too much attention to your mistake. Simply apologize and move on—but do put in the work to get it right the next time.

TIP #6: GET IT RIGHT THE NEXT TIME

So you've just messed up. Bummer. You've made your apology (ideally without sobbing); now it's time to figure out how to fix the problem. Occasional and accidental misgendering is embarrassing, but it happens, and we all do it. Repeated or intentional misgendering, without caring or doing the work to correct the error, is abuse. Here are a few pointers for getting it right the next time:

Try Again Right Away

If you mess up while in a conversation with a person, after you apologize and continue the conversation, see if you can come up with a way to use the correct term, identity, or pronoun within the next minute or two. I find this tip useful for two reasons. First, it shows the person I messed up with that I am actively working to get it right. Second, it helps me to cement the correct term, identity, or pronoun in my head.

Practice in Your Head before You Speak

Something I've learned about myself is that I can be eloquent if I have time to prepare, but I don't always think quickly on my feet. Since I know this about myself, I often run a sentence through in my head before I say it. I find this especially helpful when I am talking with a person whom I have misgendered in the past.

Imagine a Mouse

Use of the singular pronoun *they* can be especially hard if we are not used to it. My friend Eridan, whose pronoun is *they*, shared a fun tip with me to help me to get their pronouns right. They told me to imagine that they have a mouse in their pocket. Then whenever I think about Eridan I am thinking about two beings: "They are coming to dinner. Get out the tray of mini cheeses!"

Practice on Your Pet

My friend Kayden suggested that I improve the frequency of my use of singular *they* by using it on my pet. I have a male cat named Carlos. He doesn't seem to mind if I use *they* to refer to him as long as I remember to feed him on time and occasionally scratch his head. Excuse me—scratch *their* head.

DO IT ANYWAY

If a lot of this stuff is new to you, you may now be feeling a bit overwhelmed and worried that you are surely going to mess up. You will. We all do. The trick is not to put unrealistic pressure on yourself to never mess up. Try hard not to mess up, forgive yourself when you do, apologize to the person you screwed up with, and put in the work to get it right the next time. The Reverend Dr. Andrea Ayvazian, in her video "Creating Conversations: Becoming a White Ally," states: "You will do badly. Do it anyway. Do it anyway. Do not let your fear be bigger than your commitment."[3]

NOTES

1. These tips have been adapted from Out Alliance, "Being Respectful to LGBTQ+ People," training handout.
2. Human Rights Campaign, "Violence against the Transgender Community in 2018," https://www.hrc.org/resources/violence-against-the-transgender-community -in-2018.
3. Andrea Ayvazian, "Creating Conversations: Becoming a White Ally," filmed at Greenfield Community College, Greenfield, MA, November 23, 2010, https://www .youtube.com/watch?v=yXZPIIc6MkLI.

GAYDAR AND OTHER
PROBLEMATIC ASSUMPTIONS

Take all of your identities, add them up, and you get you. There has likely never been another person, in all the 108 billion years of Earth's history, whose You Soup ingredient list has been the same as yours. . . . Yet many times in your life you're going to be viewed as a one-ingredient dish.

—Sam Killermann

All lesbians have short hair, wear flannel, play softball, and drive Subarus, yes? All gay men have great fashion sense, sing show tunes, work out constantly, and say, "Guuuurrrrl!" a lot, right? Wrong. Some do, to be sure. And by the way, if you *are* a flannel-wearing, softball-playing lesbian with short hair who drives a Subaru, rock on! The purpose of this chapter is not to judge, mock, or disrespect anyone's gender expression or interests. The purpose of this chapter is to ensure that LGBTQ+ myths and stereotypes are not applied to all LGBTQ+ people and to reduce the harmful impact of myths, stereotypes, and misinformation about people in the LGBTQ+ communities.

GAYDAR

Let's start with our first goal: making sure that we are not assuming that all LG-BTQ+ people dress the same, wear their hair the same way, and have the same interests. Many readers will have, no doubt, heard the word *gaydar*. Gaydar, which combines the words *gay* and *radar*, refers to the ability some people claim to have to accurately identify a gay person simply by looking at them or talking to them.

Here is the reality of how gaydar works: We observe someone's gender expression—what they are wearing, how they style their hair, whether or not they have tattoos or body piercings, how they walk, how they talk—and we draw conclusions about whom they are attracted to. I worked at an LGBTQ+ center for fifteen years and I am here to tell you that my gaydar stinks. The reason it stinks is that there is as much variation of gender expression within the LGBTQ+ communities as there is within the straight/cisgender communities. I have no idea who is gay, lesbian, asexual, bisexual—and, I'm sorry to say, you probably don't either.

We may see a guy walking toward us with a rainbow scarf, a pride shirt, and purple hair and think to ourselves, "Gay—obviously." Then we miss the next three gay men who walk by us because they are wearing a Coors tee, a suit and tie, and construction gear. And guess what? We may even be wrong about the dude in the pride shirt! No matter what we think or hear, we cannot tell someone's orientation just by looking at them—plain and simple. Let's not even try.

LGBTQ+ MYTHS AND STEREOTYPES

LGBTQ+ myths and stereotypes can be silly: for example, "All lesbians wear Birkenstocks." But myths and stereotypes can also be incredibly hurtful: for example, "LGBTQ+ people are out to recruit others." Both types of myths and stereotypes, the silly and the hurtful, have harmful and damaging impacts on people, both within and outside of the LGBTQ+ communities.

One way that myths and stereotypes can be damaging is by preventing LGBTQ+ people from seeing accurate and varied images of other LGBTQ+

FUN FACT

When I first started working at our LGBTQ+ center, I was amused and pleased to note that I (the straight/cisgender employee) was the *only* staff member who actually wore Birkenstocks.

people, delaying their coming-out process. Even the silly stereotyping of LGBTQ+ people can be damaging. Consider a young person who is trying to figure out if she might be a lesbian, and the only thing she "knows" about lesbians is that they are all short-haired, flannel-wearing softball players. If this young person has long hair and hates sports, she may think to herself, "That's not me, so I must not be a lesbian." Rather than moving forward in her coming-out process, she is likely to go back into the stage of identity confusion, as discussed in chapter 3. My friend Matt, who is a gay man, believed the myth that gay men could not be fathers. He knew from a very early age that he wanted to be a father and so he convinced himself that he must not be gay. His understanding of himself and his coming-out process were greatly delayed by this stereotype.

Now let's take a look at some myths and stereotypes that are beyond silly. Some extremely prevalent myths and stereotypes are downright hurtful and extremely dangerous. I run an activity in one of my workshops where participants write down all of the myths and stereotypes they can think of for lesbians, gay men, bisexual or pansexual people, transgender people, and straight/cisgender allies. (Yes, there are ally myths and stereotypes too. We'll get to these in a moment.) Here are two very common and very harmful LGBTQ+ myths and stereotypes:

- Gay men are prone to pedophilia.
- If transgender women are allowed in women's restrooms they will behave inappropriately.

These myths are so familiar that they are included in this list pretty much every time I run this activity, in locations all over the United States. Participants share that they were exposed to these myths by family members, friends, teachers, faith leaders, books, movies, and the media. Whether we believe them to be true or not, they are incredibly prevalent in our society and we all seem to know them.

Some of us have done our homework and know that these hurtful myths and stereotypes are false. Unfortunately, others who do not know many LGBTQ+ people and have not researched the facts often believe these myths and stereotypes to be accurate. (We'll discuss how to respectfully challenge these myths and stereotypes in the next chapter.)

Here are some real-life examples of how these two harmful myths and stereotypes have played out in our society:

- Refusing to allow gay men to become Boy Scout leaders.
- Firing LGBTQ+ people from jobs like teaching, where they work with children.

- Fighting to keep transgender people out of restrooms that align with their gender identity.

Myths and stereotypes have a huge impact on individuals and devastating consequences for our society. As allies we must listen for them in people's questions and concerns and address them. Do your ally homework and check out the facts:

- Did you know that many studies over the years have all concluded that being gay does not make one prone to pedophilia?[1]
- Did you know that in the eighteen states that have policies allowing people to use the restroom that aligns with their gender identity, there has not been a single reported incident of a transgender person behaving inappropriately in a public restroom? There have also been no incidents of cisgender boys dressing as girls or saying that they "feel like girls" in order to access the girls' locker rooms, a common parental fear?[2]

You don't need to know all of the facts and statistics about LGBTQ+ people before you head out into the world as an ally, but it's worth having some data on the most common and hurtful myths and stereotypes in your savvy ally goody bag. Fill it with more goodies as needed as you continue on your ally journey.

NOT-SO-FUN FACT

Here is what transgender folks want to do in the bathroom: pee and peace out. I know transgender people who dehydrate themselves when they go out to social events if they are not sure they will have access to an all-gender restroom. They don't want to make other folks uncomfortable and they are worried for their own safety. Allies can help change this!

MYTHS AND STEREOTYPES ABOUT STRAIGHT/CISGENDER ALLIES

When I ask participants to list the myths and stereotypes about straight/cisgender allies I often get a blank stare. *Are* there myths and stereotypes about straight/cisgender allies? You betcha!

POP QUIZ

What is a common myth or stereotype about straight/cisgender allies to the LGBTQ+ communities? Choose all that apply.

A. Allies always have an LGBTQ+ family member or very close friend who is LGBTQ+.
B. Allies are really LGBTQ+ themselves; they just haven't come out yet.
C. Allies are awesome!

Answer: A and B

(C is a fact.)

The two most common ally myths, in my experience, are that allies must have a close friend or family member who is LGBTQ+ or they wouldn't be involved (the "it's personal" myth) and that allies are really LGBTQ+ themselves; they just haven't come out yet (the "closet case" myth). Let me share with you a little bit about the impact that these two particularly prevalent myths/stereotypes have had on me.

The first time I ever had any type of friendly relationship with out cisgender, gay, lesbian, and bisexual people was in college. (I wouldn't meet an out transgender person until 2003, when I began my work as a volunteer at our local LGBTQ+ center.) I went to college in the early 1980s, and several of my varsity volleyball teammates were lesbians. Despite my camaraderie with these teammates, it never occurred to me that I had a place at any of the "Silence = Death" rallies that were taking place on campus. I had never heard the word *ally* in the context of social justice work, and I was pretty sure I would not be welcome there. In other words, I was held back by the "it's personal" myth.

One day in the early 1990s, while I was in graduate school working toward my masters in social work, some members of the LGBTQ+ student club came into my classroom and invited all of the straight/cisgender people to attend their next meeting. After fifteen years of work at our local LGBTQ+ center, it's a bit embarrassing to admit that I needed an invitation to attend this group, but I *absolutely* needed an invitation.

After attending one meeting, a fellow student asked me, "So what's this fascination you have with lesbians all about, huh?" (wink, wink), which, I'll admit, freaked me out quite a bit. The "closet case" myth prevented me from returning to the club meetings or becoming really active for many years.

As I shared in the prologue, it wasn't until I was forty years old that I finally picked up the phone and started volunteering at our local LGBTQ+ center, launching myself into what would become a lifelong career as a straight/cisgender ally. Had those two myths about allies not gotten in the way, I likely would have started my work as an ally to the LGBTQ+ communities twenty years earlier.

How am I currently affected by these two ally myths? The "it's personal" myth is, at this point, just a fun one to bust. People often assume that I have an LGBTQ+ child. I love sharing how and why I got involved and validating the importance of the fight for LGBTQ+ rights and inclusion on its own merits.

Honestly, I still struggle with the "closet case" myth. I don't care if I am mistaken for a lesbian or a trans woman or any other identity under the LGBTQ+ umbrella. It happens all the time. I *do* mind, however, when people make the assumption that I am a closeted LGBTQ+ person or that I am confused about my own sexuality or gender. This distinction was an important discovery for me. It helped me realize that my discomfort wasn't based in prejudice or bias against LGBTQ+ people. It stemmed instead from annoyance and frustration that people may be thinking they know more about me than I do, waiting for me to figure out my "real" identity and finally come out.

Myths and stereotypes hold us all back. They are perpetuated by people both outside of and within the LGBTQ+ communities, and they are dangerous things. Listen closely, my friends. Behind almost every negative comment or concern about LGBTQ+ individuals, the savvy ally can find a hidden myth or stereotype. Hearing them is step one; debunking them is step two. (More on this coming up in the next chapter.)

INTERSECTIONALITY

For those who are unfamiliar with the word *intersectionality*, it basically means that we all have many identities that make us who we are and shape our experiences. Our age, race, body size, ability, ethnicity, class, orientation, gender identity, and gender expression are part of who we are, and they are all interconnected. You cannot simply add together the gendered experience of being a woman and the racial experience of being a person of color and come up with the lived experience of a woman of color. The ways that race and gender come together create unique experiences and produce unique societal challenges.

The word *intersectionality* was coined by Kimberlé Crenshaw in 1989. In her 2016 TED Talk "The Urgency of Intersectionality," Crenshaw talks about how a legal case was the catalyst for creating this word. The case involved Emma DeGraffenreid, an African American woman who applied for a job at a car manufacturing plant and was not hired. DeGraffenreid believed this was a case of race and gender discrimination, but the judge dismissed the suit. The judge's rationale was that the company had hired black men for many of its industrial and maintenance jobs, proving that the company wasn't discriminating on the basis of race. The company had also hired many white women for secretarial jobs, proving that the company wasn't discriminating on the basis of gender. Crenshaw said:

> I was struck by this case. It felt to me like injustice squared. So first of all, black women weren't allowed to work at the plant. Second of all, the court doubled down on this exclusion by making it legally inconsequential. And to boot, there was no name for this problem. And we all know that, where there's no name for a problem, you can't see a problem, and when you can't see a problem, you pretty much can't solve it.[3]

Crenshaw coined the term *intersectionality* to help frame DeGraffenreid's dilemma so that others could see and understand the problem. This was not simply a matter of adding up identities like a math equation and getting a simple answer. An African American woman like DeGraffenreid slipped through the cracks of the legal protections put in place for African American men and white women. The term *intersectionality* helps raise awareness that our many identities can cause multiple layers of discrimination.

Here's an example of intersectionality within the LGBTQ+ communities: Imagine an eighty-three-year-old gay man living in a senior-living facility. If we simply add the experiences of a gay man in his thirties and the experiences of an eighty-three-year-old straight man, we are unlikely to get an accurate picture of this man's life, his experiences, and the unique challenges that he faces. Because he is a gay man *and* an older adult, he has lived through a time when he saw gay men arrested for their sexual orientation, diagnosed with mental disorders simply for being themselves, and forced to undergo electroshock therapy in an attempt to "fix" them. His level of distrust of medical and mental health professionals will be heightened by these lived experiences. He is less likely to make social connections at his new living facility and more likely to hide who he is and who he has spent his life with. As professional senior caregiver Marsha Robinson says in the outstanding short film *Project Visibility*, his story would be missing.[4]

Why is a section on intersectionality included in a chapter that focuses on myths and stereotypes? Because it's a prevalent and hugely problematic myth that there is one typical way to be an LGBTQ+ person: white, able-bodied, middle-class, hearing, nonreligious, and between the ages of about sixteen and forty. But LGBTQ+ people come in all shapes, sizes, colors, ages, abilities, experiences, and backgrounds. They are grandparents, Deaf, Catholic, African American, single, homeless, low-income, cancer survivors, Republican, Muslim, polyamorous, war veterans . . . you get the idea. Their lived experiences are influenced by these intersectional identities.

One of the major barriers to having conversations about intersectionality among groups of white folks, especially when race is involved, is fear. In her brilliant book *Why Are All the Black Kids Sitting Together in the Cafeteria?*[5] Beverly Daniel Tatum talks about how white children who are curious about race and skin color get shut down by parents and educators when they ask about these differences. So white folks learn very early on that it's not okay to talk about race, and this rule is reinforced throughout our lives.

Most of the reading I have done on racial and social justice has declared that white people need to do the work to educate themselves. We cannot rely on or expect people from marginalized communities to constantly play the role of educator. But I do not see those conversations on racial advocacy happening within white communities. Mostly what I experience is a polite avoidance of the topic.

Here is a real-life example of how tongue-tied well-meaning white folks get when it comes to discussing people of color. A few years ago, I was in a pregame huddle with my all-white volleyball team. On the other side of the net, the opposing team was made up of five white guys and one black guy. (In the huddle players have about fifteen seconds to strategize before the whistle blows and they all must get on the court and play.)

Teammate #1: Hey folks. Stay true on defense. That one guy has a really good line shot and he goes there a lot.

Teammate #2: Which guy?

Teammate #1: The guy in the blue shorts.

Teammate #3: There are three guys in blue shorts.

Teammate #1: The taller guy.

Teammate #2: The guy with the cut-off sleeves?

Teammate #4: No. He's talking about the guy in the gray tee.

Teammate #2: With the stripe on his shorts?

Teammate #4: Yeah.

Teammate #2: Oh. Got it. Thanks.

All this confusion because everyone was carefully *not* saying, "the black guy." But if the other team was made up of five black guys and one white guy, I am sure the conversation would go like this:

Teammate #1: Hey folks. Stay true on defense. The white guy has a really good line shot and he goes there a lot.

Teammate #2: Got it. Thanks.

Why do people struggle when the person they are trying to identify is a person of color? I believe it is fear. Well-meaning white folks are fearful of not using the correct term (*black* or *person of color* or *African American?*), they are fearful that identifying someone by skin color is disrespectful (unless they're white), and they are fearful that someone will interpret their words as racist.

In my experience, within white communities, at best, there are conversations about a fear of accidentally saying something offensive. At worst, there is a lot of finger pointing and labeling people *racist*. We are all racist, sexist, homophobic, ageist, classist, ablest, sizest . . . and we are all fully capable of saying racist, sexist, homophobic, ageist, classist, ablest, body-shaming things. Pointing fingers gets us nowhere. As allies to any marginalized community we need to talk about these biases and focus on the impact of our words and actions, rather than labeling and shaming others. I challenge us all not to shy away from conversations about race and intersectionality, but to bravely embrace them and create spaces for honest discussions without judgment and with the assumption of good intent. The next chapter offers some suggestions for how to do that.

NOTES

1. Here are a few good articles that bust the pedophilia myth: Gregory M. Herek, "Facts about Homosexuality and Child Molestation," Sexual Orientation: Science, Education, and Policy, https://psychology.ucdavis.edu/rainbow/html/facts_molestation.html; Olga Khazan, "Milo Yiannopoulos and the Myth of the Gay Pedophile," *Atlantic*, February 21, 2107, https://www.theatlantic.com/health/archive/2017/02/milo-yiannopoulos-and-the-myth-of-the-gay-pedophile/517332/; and Gabriel Arana, "The Truth about Gay Men and Pedophilia," *INTO*, November 16, 2017, https://www.intomore.com/impact/The-Truth-About-Gay-Men-and-Pedophilia.

2. Here are a few good myth-busting articles on facility use: Amira Hasenbush, "What Does Research Suggest about Transgender Restroom Policies?" *Education Week*, June 8, 2016, https://www.edweek.org/ew/articles/2016/06/08/what-does-research -suggest-about-transgender-restroom.html; and Julie Moreau, "No Link between Trans-Inclusive Policies and Bathroom Safety, Study Finds," NBC News, September 19, 2018, https://www.nbcnews.com/feature/nbc-out/no-link-between-trans-inclusive-policies -bathroom-safety-study-finds-n911106.

3. Kimberlé Crenshaw, "The Urgency of Intersectionality," Speech given at TED-Women 2016, December 7, 2016, https://www.ted.com/talks/kimberle_crenshaw_the_ urgency_of_intersectionality?language=en.

4. AAA Project Visibility, *Project Visibility* (Boulder, CO: Boulder County Area Agency on Aging, 2004), DVD.

5. Beverly Daniel Tatum, *Why Are All the Black Kids Sitting Together in the Cafeteria?* rev. and updated ed. (New York: Basic Books, 2017).

GOOD TALK

The Art of Having Useful Conversations

If you won't make peace with different points of view, what's inclusive about your diversity?

—Irshad Manji

WE ARE ALL RESISTANT LEARNERS

Before we dive into how to be an effective agent for change as savvy allies and how we can effectively educate others, let's think for a moment about how we ourselves learn. I believe that the best way to move people along in their journey of understanding, accepting, and eventually appreciating people who are unlike themselves is to remind ourselves what things are like when we are in the hot seat as the learners.

All of us have a lump of knowledge, if you will, in our brains. This is stuff that we "know" to be true. (Please note the quotation marks here.) This lump of knowledge is information that we have gathered over our lifetime to make sense of the world.

Now let's look at what happens when we get a new piece of information that doesn't jibe with what we have going on in our lump of knowledge. Typically, we think about that new piece of information for a moment before dismissing it with a "nah." This is good, and this is as it should be. Think about the consequences of living in a world where everyone took new information, the second they got it, and replaced what they had known up to that point in time. Life would be absolute chaos.

Imagine a child trying to learn where babies come from, gathering disparate information from multiple sources.

> Mom: "When a mommy and a daddy love each other they kiss and make a baby." (Got it!)
>
> Aunt Sophie: "The stork drops the baby down the chimney." (Understood.)
>
> Best friend's big brother: "I heard the dad sticks the baby in the mom with his penis!" (Gross! But okay . . .)
>
> Grandpa: "You can buy 'em on Amazon." (Wow! They really *do* sell everything.)

No, it's a wonderful thing that humans are resistant learners. We must be. There is a lot of bad information out there and we don't want to allow that stuff into our wonderful brains. We've worked hard to acquire our lump of knowledge, and we have to protect it.

But let's say that over time, we continue to hear this new piece of information: perhaps in the media, perhaps during conversations with trusted and respected friends. Now we have some evidence that this new piece of information may be worth looking at more seriously. We ponder it. Perhaps we do a little research of our own. Eventually we may even decide that this new piece of information is right and valid—more right and valid even than the conflicting piece of information we have been holding in our own lump of knowledge. And then we do something amazing: We replace the old piece with the new piece.

The point is that learning is a process. Here, for your entertainment, is an embarrassing example of a time when I went through this process. I managed to make it well into my young adulthood "knowing" that the thing that you fill with leaves and push around your yard is called a "wheelbarrel." One evening over dinner, my sister Julie offered up a new piece of information: She claimed that the word was actually *wheelbarrow*. I immediately resisted this new information. Here was my thought process: "What the heck is a barrow? Wheelbarrel makes sense! It's basically a barrel on wheels. The original wheelbarrels probably *were* literally barrels on wheels. In addition, I have lived for more than two decades and never, to my knowledge, have I seen *wheelbarrow* written in any book, or I would have been aware of this ridiculous word. She must be wrong."

My learning process continued and included receiving affirmation from others that my sister was correct; pondering the likelihood of actually winning an argument with my sister, who is always right (super irritating, but true);

and finally trudging over to the dictionary and looking the word up. (A funny side note is that when I recently shared this story with a twenty-four-year-old coworker, he also could not believe the word was *wheelbarrow* and the process started all over for him.)

Replacing information that we "know" is even harder when we have "known" it for a long period of time and when the people around us in our community also "know" it. If the people we trust (our parents, our friends, our teachers, our faith leaders) have all taught us that being LGBTQ+ is a disease or is immoral, we are extremely unlikely to alter that assessment of LGBTQ+ people without a great deal of respectful conversation and getting to know many healthy, happy, well-adjusted, and kind LGBTQ+ people.

We should think about the conversations related to LGBTQ+ people that we will doubtless take part in after reading this book not as a way to change minds but as opportunities to exchange ideas and to plant seeds to ponder. This will not only help us with our messaging and tone, but it will also take the pressure off of our shoulders to come up with that perfectly clear, informative, succinct, "angels singing in the background" response that will immediately change the mind of the incredibly stubborn person in front of us.

During my work as an LGBTQ+ educator I am frequently asked, "My [fill in the blank—usually a relative] is *so* homophobic! What can I say to change [his/her/their] mind?" The answer, of course, is that there *is* no one thing you can say to change someone's mind. What we *can* do is have respectful conversations where we share our thoughts and experiences in ways that open people's ears for listening to and learning from each other.

Try and avoid the common pattern of half listening, labeling the person or the behavior, then reacting. For example:

Person A: My son's teacher read his class a story about two dads. It made me uncomfortable. I'm worried my son—

Person B: OMG! Are you serious? That is *so* homophobic!

Instead, try to fully listen, ponder, then discuss. For example:

Person A: My son's teacher read his class a story about two dads. It made me uncomfortable. I'm worried my son will ask me questions about being gay or transgender and I won't know how to answer them.

Person B: Oh yeah. I get that. I also like being prepared with appropriate and well-thought-out responses when my kids ask me questions. I bet I can find some good resources for you about how to talk with your kids about LGBTQ+ people and families. Would you like me to take a look?

PUTTING OURSELVES IN THE HOT SEAT

As you move along on your journey as an effective ally and educator, it's important to continue to come back to your experiences as a learner. Ask yourself, "If I am the person whose lump of knowledge is being challenged, what will shut me down to the conversation and what will open my ears to new thoughts and ideas?"

Think about a time when someone called you out on something you said or did—in other words, you said or did something that someone else found offensive and they brought it to your attention. Was the interaction effective? What worked and what didn't work in this interaction? When I ask people to offer their thoughts on what has and hasn't worked in these situations, I typically get a list that looks like this:

Didn't Work
Yelling
Calling me out in front of a bunch of people
Blasting me on social media
Labeling me and/or the behavior/comment (e.g., racist, sexist, homophobic)

Worked
Focusing on why the comment made them unhappy
Speaking to me in private
Sharing that they had made a similar mistake once too (i.e., making themselves vulnerable)
Making it clear that they were having the conversation with me because they valued our relationship or friendship

When we yell, shame people in public, or label people or behaviors, we create a situation where the other person is likely to respond by becoming defensive and offended. In addition, the conversation will likely focus not on the real issue (i.e., why the comment upset us) but instead on whether or not the comment was, in fact, sexist, racist, or homophobic. The focus will be on the intent, not the impact.

A NIGHT OUT WITH LOU THE LUNCHROOM AIDE

A few years ago, I was facilitating a workshop for a group of school lunchroom aides. It was a mandatory training for them, so I went into it knowing that I

<hr>

POP QUIZ

Select all statements that are true.

A. Christians are anti-LGBTQ+.
B. All religions and faith communities are anti-LGBTQ+.
C. Many religions and faith communities welcome and support LGBTQ+ individuals.
D. You cannot be LGBTQ+ and also be religious.

Answer: C

It's a harmful myth that all religions and faith communities are anti-LGBTQ+. Many religions and faith communities, including Christians, have created wonderfully welcoming and affirming spaces for LGBTQ+ individuals and their families. One thing that really surprised me when I first began my work as an ally was how many LGBTQ+ people were people of faith and were very active in their faith communities. It's true that some religions have anti-LGBTQ+ beliefs, but not all do, and many are becoming more inclusive with time.

<hr>

wouldn't necessarily be preaching to the choir. Partway through the presentation, a man—whom I will call Lou—raised his hand and asked a question. His manner was so quiet and calm that it took me a moment to realize that he was an unhappy camper. Essentially his question to me was, "You have just come into my space to share your agenda and your beliefs. Now may I come into your space at the LGBTQ+ center to share my agenda and beliefs as a Christian man?"

How did I respond to Lou, my respectful but unhappy camper?

1. I took a deep breath. I dislike conflict and taking a deep breath always helps me relax.

2. I thanked him. I told him that I appreciated his honesty and I stated that he was probably not the only person in the room who felt that way or who had those concerns.

3. I reassured him that I was not there to try and force anyone to change their beliefs. We all come together at school or work from very different backgrounds and with different beliefs, and we must all work together in a respectful way.

4. I clarified what my agenda was: that I was working toward making our schools safe and welcoming for everyone. This meant that schools must

be safe and welcoming for the kid who has two moms *and* for the kid whose parents are teaching them that being gay is a sin. Lunchroom aides, other school staff, teachers, and administrators need to create a space where both of those children feel safe and respected, and they need the tools to do that. That was my agenda.

My response did what I hoped it would do. Lou and I continued to talk about this topic for a few minutes, modeling a respectful and professional exchange. Although Lou and I felt very differently about LGBTQ+ people, through our conversation we were able to find some common ground. We agreed that we both wanted schools to be safe places for all children. Through this respectful exchange, I also let the participants know that I was open to hearing from people with different perspectives.

When the workshop was over, I did something I had never done before: I invited a participant (Lou) out to dinner. I thought to myself, "This man sat through my workshop feeling super uncomfortable and probably pretty pissed off that he was being forced to attend, and yet he was so incredibly respectful in his response to me. He didn't yell or show anger in any way. This is someone I would like to spend more time with." I rarely get a chance to talk with people who are opposed to the work that I do and who are willing to share that in a calm and respectful way. I suspected that Lou and I could manage to have a pretty cool conversation, given the chance.

Lou was uncomfortable with the idea of dinner with me, he confessed to me later, so he went to his priest for advice about whether to accept the invitation or not. His priest told him he saw no harm in it, so a few weeks later Lou and I met at the Cheesecake Factory for food and a chat. This dinner stands out as one of the most memorable moments of my career in LGBTQ+ education. Here are a couple key things that I learned from Lou:

- I needed to be more careful with my language and clarify my goals with audiences, especially when attendance was required and I knew there would be people in the room who did not want to be there. Lou was very concerned about what I meant by "getting into the schools." He believed my goal was to talk with elementary school children about sex. (The confusion over orientation and intimate behaviors rears its ugly head again!) Lou told me it felt like "indoctrination" of children to him and reminded him of the Nazis.
- Knowing that this was a mandatory workshop and that some folks would be very uncomfortable with the topic, I should have made a bigger effort to welcome everyone by saying something like this early on: "I know we

are all coming from different places, that we all have different beliefs, and that some of us may feel very uncomfortable even being here today. I want you to know that I welcome you to voice different perspectives if they are respectfully shared."

Lou told me that he also got quite a bit out of the dinner conversation and that he left feeling more comfortable with the work that our agency was doing. And I was right—neither of us raised our voices or got angry. In fact, it was such an enjoyable dinner that, as we hugged good-bye, Lou said he would welcome another opportunity to get together and talk.

Probably the biggest takeaway for me was that we had so much in common! We both wanted many of the same things for our children and for our world; we were just coming at it from different angles. I am pretty sure that neither of us budged an inch on our core beliefs—we are resistant learners, after all—but we both left with some major respect for each other and a much better understanding of where the other person was coming from. And who knows what potential seeds of change we planted in each other?

TIPS FOR RESPECTFUL COMMUNICATION

How do we have respectful and useful conversations with people who have opposing views and beliefs? Over the years I have compiled a list of the most effective tips for having conversations in a way that everyone involved is less likely to get defensive and more likely to be open to new ideas. I used almost all of these techniques during my conversation with Lou.[1]

Assume Good Intent

If a person uses an icky, outdated term or makes a comment that rubs you the wrong way, assume that they did not intend to be hurtful. This simple assumption will take you so very far in your efforts to have respectful conversations. In fact, it's the founding principle on which all of my educational efforts are built. Assuming that the person has simply not gotten the memo on the most updated and respectful terms—which is most likely true—will set the tone for a wonderful interaction.

Please do keep in mind that assuming good intent should not take the place of important conversations; it is simply setting the tone for important conversations. Assuming good intent should never be used to excuse disrespectful behaviors or rationalize hurtful comments. It is not a free pass for a person to say and do whatever they want because they "didn't mean it that way." Your conversations should still focus on the impact of people's words and actions rather than the intent. However, you will shame and frighten people into silence if you do not allow them to use the language and the information they have to ask questions and to discuss concepts.

This approach is very personal to me. I became an active ally in 2003 knowing almost nothing about the LGBTQ+ communities. I used the wrong terms. I asked inappropriate questions. I messed up royally. Fifteen years of professional work as an ally to the LGBTQ+ communities would never have happened if people had not assumed that I had good intentions and that I just didn't know any better.

Avoid Labeling the Comment or Behavior

Many social justice educators agree that labeling people (e.g., "You're homophobic") is not an effective way to get people to listen or change their behavior. The popular solution seems to be to label the behavior instead (e.g., "What you just said was homophobic"). I'm going to go one step further and suggest that we don't label anything at all.

Let's imagine you and I are having lunch and I say, "That's so gay!" Unless I am talking about the upcoming Pride parade, that comment is not cool. If you now say to me, "That comment was homophobic," most likely I will get super defensive and the conversation will veer off on a tangent about why the comment was or wasn't homophobic rather than focusing on the real issue at hand, which is that the comment made you feel yucky.

HELPFUL HINT

If you just said to yourself, "Ugh. This woman is being *way* too sensitive. No one means 'That's so gay' in a hurtful way," I hope you will take a look at the five-and-a-half-minute video by the fabulous Ash Beckham called "I Am SO GAY," available at http://www.ignitetalks.io/videos/i-am-so-gay. If it does nothing else, it's sure to make you literally LOL.

Use "I" Statements

One of the ways we can focus the conversation on what is important—the impact the comment had on you—is to use "I" statements or other language that focuses on you and how the comment made you feel.

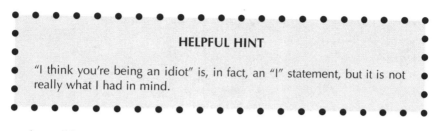

HELPFUL HINT

"I think you're being an idiot" is, in fact, an "I" statement, but it is not really what I had in mind.

A possible response to "That's so gay" is, "I would love it if you used a different word. I'm sure you didn't mean it in a hurtful way" (like how I squeezed in the first tip?) "but it upsets me when people use the word *gay* in a negative way like that."

Find Common Ground

If you have ever struggled with inclusive language or understanding a concept yourself, now is a great time to bring it up. This will put you and the person you are talking with on the same level. For example: "You know, I used to say, 'That's so gay' all the time. Then a friend said something to me that made me stop and think about what I was saying." Another way to connect or find common ground with someone is to start by acknowledging that it's hard to keep up with changes in language and terminology. For example, you might start a conversation with, "I know this stuff can be super confusing."

Try the "Switch It" Technique

The "switch it" technique is a fantastic educational tool. I have already used it several times in this book. It works well as a self-help tool to determine whether or not a question is respectful and appropriate. Not sure if it's okay to ask your transgender coworker whether or not she takes hormones? Try switching it. Would you ask a cisgender coworker about their medications? This is also a great savvy ally tool for helping to educate others.

The 2008 Think Before You Speak campaign used the "switch it" technique beautifully. Through this campaign, people created advertisements that explained that the word *gay* shouldn't be used to replace the words *bad* or *pathetic*. The ads made the case by switching the situation and replacing *gay* with other words. One ad features comedian Wanda Sykes. She is at a restaurant and hears three teenage boys saying that something is "so gay." So she walks over and tells them they shouldn't call something *gay* when they actually mean that it's silly or ridiculous because it's insulting. She explains that it's like if she thought the pepper shaker was silly and she said, "Man, this pepper shaker is so sixteen-year-old boy with a cheesy mustache."

The "switch it" technique can also work well for larger administrative concerns. Many administrators, supervisors, and teachers who know exactly how they would handle a bullying situation or a workplace conflict that involves race or ability are often completely discombobulated when it comes to handling situations involving LGBTQ+ people. I believe this goes back to that misunderstanding that being LGBTQ+ is all about sexual behaviors rather than about families, whom we love, and who we are.

If a friend is struggling with a situation with an employee who says they do not feel comfortable sharing an office with a gay coworker and your friend doesn't know how to handle the situation, try switching it to a situation with an identity where your friend *does* know how they would handle it. What if this employee said they didn't feel comfortable sharing an office with a black coworker, or a Muslim coworker, or a Deaf coworker? If they know how they would handle that situation, you can assure them that they have the tools they need to handle the LGBTQ+ concern. A few years ago, in a local school district, a father met with a high school principal to demand that his son be removed from a class that was taught by a gay teacher. The principal picked up a piece of paper and a pen and said, "Let's see. What if the teacher is a person of color? Is that okay? What if the teacher is Jewish? Is that okay?" And then he crumpled up the piece of paper and said, "Nope. We're not doing this. Your son is in that class." This story has a beautiful ending: The gay teacher ended up being the boy's all-time favorite teacher and the father later returned to thank the principal for what he had done.

Listen for Those Myths and Stereotypes

We read about the impact of LGBTQ+ myths and stereotypes in the last chapter. Well, now is our opportunity to listen for them and address them. Hidden within a lot of people's concerns about LGBTQ+ people are myths, stereotypes, and misinformation. Lou had brought with him the myth that LGBTQ+ people (and apparently even straight, cisgender allies) have an "agenda" that involves recruiting and indoctrinating children. He came right out and stated his concern, so it was easy to address.

Sometimes the comment or concern is more subtle, as with the father who didn't want his son taught by a gay teacher. Let's say this father brings his concern to you and you respond by saying, "Huh. I don't feel that way. I wouldn't have a problem with my son being taught by a gay teacher." That shows support for the LGBTQ+ communities, but does not actually addressing the underlying concern.

A better approach is to encourage this dad to share what concerns him about his son having a gay teacher so you can listen for and address the myths behind the fears. A neat trick I learned while getting my master's degree in social work is that people get more defensive if you start a question with "why" than they do if you start with any other question word. So rather than, "Why would you say that?" try, "What makes you say that?" Or you can simply say, "I'd love to hear a little more about your concerns."

If you are successful and you have sniffed out the root of the problem, then you have probably figured out that this man's lump of knowledge includes some—or many—myths about gay men. Perhaps he truly believes that gay men are prone to pedophilia, are bad role models for boys, are out to recruit boys into the gay "lifestyle," are extremely promiscuous, or a combination of all of these.

Now you have a choice. You can think to yourself, "Zowie! This guy is a flaming homophobe!" Or you can empathize and admit to yourself that this man is doing exactly what a parent should do: He is being protective of his child and trying to keep his child safe in what he perceives to be a potentially dangerous situation. Thinking of this man as a good and caring father who just has some misinformation—instead of as a homophobic bonehead—is the best way to begin your respectful conversation.

Utilizing the tips above, you can now move into a respectful, nonjudgmental conversation where you both exchange your thoughts and experiences. This father can share where he has gotten his information about gay men and you can share your own experiences and information. If you have had good experiences with gay teachers, share those personal experiences. If you've done your homework and you have some actual myth-busting data to whip out of your savvy ally goodie bag, share that.

You won't have all of the facts available at all times for every myth, stereotype, or misunderstanding, so don't feel like you have to before you can go out into the world and have conversations. We all learn as we go. Continue to educate yourself and become familiar with the facts, and don't be afraid to return to a conversation later when you feel better informed.

Be Aware of Your Hot Buttons

We are not robots. We are humans. We will have emotional reactions to comments and questions, and we need to be aware of those and forgive ourselves. Hot-button issues are those comments or questions that get us especially riled up, heated, angry, and tongue-tied. When our hot buttons are pressed, we are less likely to assume good intent and more likely to respond with anger and sarcasm.

Knowing which questions and topics are personal hot buttons for you is an important step toward being an effective educator. Once you are aware of your hot buttons, you can practice appropriate responses when you are calm and in your own space. If you are not yet aware of your hot buttons and a comment or question arises that causes the steam to pour from your nose and ears, a good strategy is to buy yourself some time. You might say something like, "I need to ponder that for a bit. I'll get back to you," or, "Ooooh! Pizza! Hold that thought. I'll be back in a few!"

As I mentioned earlier in the book, I am not good at thinking on my feet under pressure, but I usually get there eventually. I have been known to come back to conversations weeks later, with statements like, "Hey—remember that conversation we had a few weeks ago where you were asking me why there isn't a Straight Pride parade? Well, I've been pondering that, and I came up with a few thoughts." (Not sure how *you* would respond to this question? See chapter 9 for more on addressing common questions.)

I also firmly believe that there are no expiration dates on apologies. I have come back months later to conversations that are weighing heavily on my mind so that I could offer apologies where I may have messed up or responded too heatedly. I can't think of a single time when one of my belated apologies didn't end in a wonderful conversation and a stronger relationship.

AN ALLY'S GIFT

If done well, with a big heart, a nonjudgmental attitude, and (if we can pull it off without being snarky) a sense of humor, allies can offer a wonderful gift to others. Allies can connect with people like themselves, offering a space where people can ask foolish questions, use outdated words, and mess up royally without feeling like jerks. Our small, under-$10 gift is sharing information that we have that someone else might not, but our big, full-paycheck gift is creating a space where we can listen and share without anyone feeling shamed or judged— something we need a whole lot more of in this world.

NOTE

1. Many of these tips originally came from Scott Fearing's work at OutFront Minnesota and his *Successful GLBT Education: A Manual* (Minneapolis: OutFront Minnesota, 1996).

COMMON BLOOPERS

The only real mistake is the one from which we learn nothing.

—John Powell

"**J**ust tell me what not to say." This plea is so common that even though I am not focusing heavily on vocabulary in this book, I decided to add a chapter on outdated terms and cultural faux pas. However, just as individuals embrace different identities and define them in a variety of ways, individuals also have differing opinions about what is offensive and what is not. So before diving into some common bloopers, I want to acknowledge that not everyone thinks these are bloopers. These are simply respectful language choices to make if you have no other information about how a person identifies.

TRANSGENDER IS AN ADJECTIVE

People get very creative with the word *transgender* and the shortened version *trans*. In most situations creativity is a great thing. In this case it's not, and some of the creative variations of the word *transgender* can be quite offensive.

The words *transgender* and *trans* are adjectives: descriptive words that describe a noun. The same is true for the words *gay* and *queer*, but the words *transgender* and *trans* seem to get misused the most.

Correct	*Incorrect*
A transgender man	A transgender
Trans folks	The transgenders
They are a transgender person.	They are a transgendered person.

Another creative variation of the word *transgender* is the incorrect word *transgendering*. People transition; they don't transgender.

People also confuse the terms *transgender man* and *transgender woman*. They are unsure which is which. Here is a tip that helped me when I was first figuring this out: It would be very unusual for a person to embrace an identity term that had the wrong gender word in it. So the identity is, very simply put, where the person is going, not where they are coming from. Let's look at the wonderful Laverne Cox. She was assigned male at birth, but she is a woman. My guess is she wouldn't want the words *male* or *man* included in any part of her identity. She is a transgender woman.

AVOID THE WORDS *PREFERRED* AND *PREFERENCE*

For many years it was common to ask people to share their preferred pronoun. You are likely to still see this verbiage on forms. I and many others have moved away from the word *preferred*, instead simply saying, "What pronoun do you use?" The word *preferred* implies that the person has selected it, rather than that it is something that's part of their identity. We can use the "switch it" technique to better understand this concept: You would probably never ask a cisgender person what their preferred pronoun is. It's just their pronoun. Asking for preferred pronoun also implies that the person prefers a specific pronoun but that any pronoun will do, when typically this is not the case.

You should also avoid the words *preferred* and *preference* when talking about whom people are attracted to. I often hear people say, "That's his sexual preference." It is more respectful to say, "That's his sexual orientation." Once again, the word *preference* implies that someone's attraction is a choice rather than a part of who they are. Listen to the difference in these two sentences: "She is attracted to women" and "She prefers to sleep with women." The second comment sounds like, "Yeah, she prefers to sleep with women, but if there are none around, anyone will do." Being intentional with your language and avoiding the words *preferred* and *preference* in these contexts is a great way for you to indicate to others that people do not choose their orientation or gender.

USE LANGUAGE THAT REFLECTS TRANSITIONING AS A LIFELONG JOURNEY

Avoid the phrase "completed transition" or any other language that implies that a transitioning person is "done," like a cinnamon roll in the oven. I have never had a single transgender person ever tell me that their transition was done. Transitioning is a lifelong journey. Every trans person has their own unique decisions to make about the process, and these decisions may change throughout their lifetime. Their transitioning experience may or may not include legal name changes (on some or all documents), hormone therapies, and/or various surgeries. Each

POP QUIZ

When should we change the name and pronoun, during everyday interactions, with a coworker who is transitioning?

A. When the coworker tells us to please use their new name and pronoun.
B. When the coworker tells us to please use their new name and pronoun and their name has been legally changed.
C. When the coworker tells us to please use their new name and pronoun, their name has been legally changed, they have completed a medical transition, and they are wearing their "Done!" sticker.

Answer: A

Ideally, the leadership and human resources departments at your workplace will have met with the transitioning employee to create a workplace transitioning plan that includes decisions involving the sharing of their new name and pronouns with others. As coworkers, our job is to use the new name and pronoun when told to do so. The legal status of a coworker's new name and their medical choices do not and should not matter to us.

Here comes the wonderfully useful "switch it" technique! Can you imagine saying these things to a coworker?

"Congratulations on your marriage! I hear you have asked us to use a new last name. Has your name actually been legally changed? 'Cause if not, I think I'm gonna wait until that paperwork comes through before I stop using your old name."
"Hey, Tanya, my wife is thinking of having a hysterectomy. Do you still have your uterus?"

individual must decide for themselves what is right for them, what they can afford, and what new care is necessary as their body ages and changes.

Transitioning can be a daunting, time-consuming process and a huge financial burden. Many individuals cannot afford the hormone therapies or surgeries they need. Legal name changes are complicated and difficult to access for those who work a nine-to-five weekday job, and can be a financial burden as well. Other reasons why a transgender person might not legally change their name have to do with safety, insurance coverage, age, and their support system.

For all of these reasons listed above, legal restrictions for transgender people contingent on a person's transition being "done"—which are not uncommon—are extremely unfair. For example, many states require transgender individuals to show medical proof that they have had specific surgeries before they can apply for a name change on their birth certificate. As allies we can help educate others on the realities of the transitioning process, the fact that not all transgender people transition, and that a person's transition is never really "done."

The Human Rights Campaign (HRC) website at https://www.hrc.org/resources/workplace-gender-transition-guidelines is a great resource for best-practice tips and guidelines on transitioning in the workplace.

BE IN THE PRESENT

If you stay focused on the present, then you should be able to follow these simple rules when you talk with and about transgender people:

- Always use people's current name and pronoun, even when talking about someone's past.
- Do not ask what a transgender person's name used to be.
- Do not ask to see a pretransition photo.

For many transgender individuals, the time before they transitioned was a painful one when they were forced to express themselves in a way that felt wrong. Using an old name or pronoun for a transgender person, asking what their name used to be, or asking to see a photo of them before they transitioned may be asking them to go back to a very unhappy place.

If you must refer to a transgender person's past, and you are not outing them inappropriately by doing so, here are a couple of respectful communication tips for doing it correctly:

- Rather than saying, "When you were a boy . . ." or "When you were a girl . . .," say, "Before you transitioned . . ."

- Rather than saying that someone was "born a boy" or "born a girl," refer to the sex they were "assigned at birth." In chapter 2, when I defined the term *cisgender*, I didn't say, "A cisgender person is a person whose biological sex matches their gender identity." I said, "A cisgender person is a person whose sex assigned at birth matches their gender identity." If what we are referring to is the doctor's peek between a newborn's legs and not a person's chromosomes, hormone levels, and reproductive organs, then saying "sex assigned at birth" rather than "biological sex" is not only more respectful, it's more accurate as well.

DON'T ASK A GAY COUPLE WHICH ONE IS THE MAN AND WHICH ONE IS THE WOMAN

This common question assumes that all relationships must mirror the masculine man/feminine woman structure that's typical of conventional straight couples. My friend Sam, a gay cisgender man, shares his feelings about this question beautifully:

> Huh? Are they asking who cleans the house or who is top and who is bottom in the bedroom? Are they asking if one of us pretends to be a woman, or wishes that he was? This is such a loaded question! It assumes that all legitimate couples fit into a binary gender-role division. All partnerships, whether they are gay or straight, bring together people who have a combination of skills, interests, styles, and personalities. The answer is, of course, that we're both "the man" because we are both men! But more importantly, we are both ourselves and not trying to match anyone's definition of what it means to be a man but our own.

USE THIS TERM INSTEAD OF THAT ONE

In this section I will share some outdated terms that are generally falling out of favor. There are still some LGBTQ+ people who use them to refer to themselves, and we should obviously mirror those terms back when we hear them being used. In general, however, it's a respectful starting point to swap the outdated term for the new term as listed here.

Use *Transgender* Instead of *Transsexual*

Transsexual is a dated term that seems to be falling out of favor, especially with younger people. Some people dislike this word because it has the word *sexual* in it, which tends to reinforce the mistaken notion that all things LGBTQ+ are about sex. Others feel that the word *transsexual* is inaccurate, because the term focuses on a person's sex rather than their gender identity. In addition, the term *transsexual* can hold a negative connotation as it was originally used within psychological communities to diagnose people with mental disorders. Most people now use the term *transgender* or simply *trans*.

The word *transgender* can be used as an individual identity, but it can also be used as an umbrella term referring to a whole community. People who fall under the transgender umbrella are folks I lovingly refer to as "gender outlaws." (Thank you, Kate Bornstein!) Gender outlaws are a beautiful array of individuals who do not conform to society's rigid gender roles and expectations. This can include people who are trans women, nonbinary, trans men, genderqueer, gender-fluid, agender, Two-Spirit, gender expansive, gender nonconforming, and so much more.

Use *Cross-Dresser* Instead of *Transvestite*

Transvestite is another outdated term. Cross it out in your head and replace it with *cross-dresser*. A cross-dresser is a person who enjoys wearing clothing that society doesn't consider appropriate for their gender. Cross-dressing is about a person's gender expression. It tells us nothing about their gender identity or their orientation.

Use *Gay* Instead of *Homosexual*

Many people dislike the word *homosexual* for the same reasons that people dislike the term *transsexual*: It has the word *sexual* in it, and it was originally used within psychological communities to diagnose people with mental disorders.

POP QUIZ

Which two countries were the first to declare that homosexuality was not a mental disorder?

A. The United States and Canada
B. New Zealand and Australia
C. Sweden and Denmark

Answer: B

The Royal Australian and New Zealand College of Psychiatrists Federal Council removed homosexuality from its list of mental illnesses in October 1973.

Use *Typical* Instead of *Normal*

When we are discussing gender identities, gender expressions, or biological sexes that are common or expected, it's respectful to use the word *typical*. Try to avoid the word *normal*. The opposite of normal is abnormal, which has a pretty icky connotation.

Use *Intersex* Instead of *Hermaphrodite*

As we discussed in chapter 4, *hermaphrodite* is a dated and inaccurate term that pathologizes natural body variation. When talking about intersex individuals, also avoid words like *condition* or *disorder*. These words imply that being intersex is wrong or unnatural. Intersex people have beautiful and natural biological variations.

Use *Different Sex* or *Gender* Instead of *Opposite Sex* or *Gender*

Remember the advanced "-Ness" model that Sam Killermann created to get away from opposites? Instead of *opposite*, try *different*, as in, "I'm attracted to people of a different gender than me." If you're straight, you could change the sentence "I'm only attracted to the opposite sex" to "I'm only attracted to [fill in the blank with *men* or *women*]."

AVOID THESE WORDS ALTOGETHER

Lifestyle

Living in the woods without electricity and a flush toilet is a lifestyle. Being LGBTQ+ is not. It's just who someone is. There is no gay lifestyle just as there is no straight lifestyle.

Tranny, *Fag*, and *Dyke*

Although these words may be thrown around jokingly within community, they are not okay for others to use. (See chapter 9 for a detailed discussion of why this is so.) As allies, we should help others understand that these words are incredibly offensive.

POP QUIZ

You've just finished reading this chapter, realized that you have been guilty of one or more of these bloopers, and you feel like poop. You should:

A. Tell yourself you're a terrible person and a hopeless ally and close the book.

B. Tell yourself that it's okay to make these mistakes. You get a pass because you are an ally.

C. Remember that we all make mistakes. Allow yourself to be raggedy, but do put in the work to move forward.

Answer: C

Allow yourself to be raggedy, but please don't assume that you get a special pass just because you are an ally. You must hold yourself accountable for your language and behaviors just like everyone else.

One of the most horrendous examples I've encountered of a straight/cisgender person using what they considered to be their "special ally pass" happened at a workshop I was facilitating for a group of teachers at a school. My cofacilitator, a young trans man, had attended the school as a student, so several of the teachers in the audience knew him before he had transitioned. As I chatted with one of the teachers before the workshop, she continually referred to my cofacilitator using his old pronoun. When I said to her, "Oh, hey, I just want to remind you that he is now using *he* as his pronoun," she said, "Oh, it's okay for *me* to say that because we go way back!"

Even if we have lots of LGBTQ+ friends, allies don't get a special pass to be disrespectful or hurtful with our language. In fact, just the opposite is true. We should be modeling the most inclusive and supportive language we possibly can so that, like superstar Laverne Cox, we can be possibility models.

So remember that we *all* make mistakes. When you do, apologize, forgive yourself, and put in the work to get it right the next time.

BE EXCELLENT TO YOURSELF

Still feel like poop? You're a tough customer. Let's take care of you. How would you respond to your best friend if they just blooped? You would probably say something like, "Hey! This stuff is new for a lot of us. You didn't know. Now, moving forward you've got new information, which is great! It's okay, my friend. You're awesome!" Now please say that to yourself.

Part III

TAKING ACTION TO CREATE MORE INCLUSIVE SPACES

STRAIGHT PRIDE PARADES AND SPECIAL SNOWFLAKES

Addressing Common Questions

Instead of wondering why there isn't a straight pride, be grateful you have never needed one. Celebrate with us.

—Anthony Venn-Brown

During my fifteen years as an LGBTQ+ educator, some questions have taken me by surprise, like:

Do you think that homosexuality is caused by aluminum cans?
Does your husband know you are a lesbian?

One of my favorites was from a participant at a diversity conference who wandered into my the Power of the Ally training and asked:

Aren't we going to be talking about military strategies?

Other questions are extremely common and seem to come up again and again. As allies, we should be familiar with these common questions and be prepared with appropriate responses. Following are nine very common questions that are well worth your savvy ally time to become familiar with, as well as some suggested responses.

AREN'T WE IN A GOOD PLACE NOW WITH LGBTQ+ RIGHTS AND INCLUSION? WHAT'S LEFT TO DO?

I believe the myth that LGBTQ+ people now have all of their rights in place and are mostly being treated with equality and equity holds back a lot of folks who might otherwise be more involved as allies. The answer is no. We are not yet in a good place with LGBTQ+ rights and inclusion. There is still a lot to do.

In response to this question, I like to share that LGBTQ+ individuals do not have legal protections in place on a federal level in the United States. In about half of the states, it's still legal to fire someone from their job, kick them out of public housing, and refuse to serve them in a restaurant because of their orientation.[1] This affects our lesbian, gay, bisexual, and pansexual friends. In about two-thirds of the states this type of legal discrimination still exists against transgender people.[2] Lots of folks do not know this, and it's well worth sharing. In some countries being LGBTQ+ is a crime punishable by arrest or in some cases even death. Be familiar with the legal rights and protections in your state or country. *Wikipedia* has a very useful page that will help you find the most updated information on LGBTQ+ rights by country and territory.[3]

Sharing information about current rights for LGBTQ+ people is what I call a "big picture" response. A personal response can also work well to answer this question. The way I offer a personal response is by sharing some examples of stuff I can do as a straight, cisgender person that my LGBTQ+ friends cannot. A few examples are:

- I can find a restroom to pee in safely and conveniently pretty much anywhere I go.
- My husband and I can hold hands and walk pretty much anywhere without fearing for our safety.
- In an emergency medical situation, I know I will not have to worry about being treated respectfully or being placed in a ward that doesn't match my gender identity.
- When I was growing up, I saw straight, cisgender people like me represented constantly in the school curriculum, in books, and in movies.

These are the smaller daily realities that help people understand the work that still needs to happen to create a world that is more inclusive to LGBTQ+ people. A good ally exercise is to move through your day and ask yourself, "How would this situation be different if I were [fill in the blank: a trans woman of color, a Deaf gay man, a sixteen-year-old asexual boy, etc.]?" Use those examples to highlight things you can do with ease that others can't.

I JUST TREAT EVERYONE THE SAME; WHAT'S WRONG WITH THAT?

Lots of folks think that if they are treating everyone the same then they are putting in enough work toward creating an inclusive world; they feel that they do not need to learn about different groups of people in order to be fair and just. This comment is similar to: "I don't see color." Both of these are hot-button comments for many people within marginalized communities. What a great opportunity for an ally! We are in a prime position to step in, assume good intent, meet people where they are, share what we know, and offer them a safe place to figure it all out.

So an excellent place for an ally to begin when we hear this question is to take a deep breath and remember that it is coming from a kind place. The people I have talked with who have asked this question are folks who think that treating everyone the same is the best way to fix an unfair and biased world. Our job is to thank them for their kindness and their commitment to making the world a better place, and then help them learn an even better way.

There are two strategies I use to help people understand that we need to do more than simply treat everyone the same. One is explaining the difference between equality and equity. The other is helping people understand that we all have our own experiences as intersectional beings and that treating everyone the same is at best unproductive and at worst offensive.

First, let's think about how we can effectively educate others about the distinction between equality and equity. I find that sharing concrete examples and personal stories, either my own or borrowed stories that I have permission to share, is one of the most effective ways to help people understand concepts. Below are two examples of how a person might explain the difference between equality and equity to someone. The first involves defining the terms. The second gives an example of how the two concepts can play out in the world. Which do you think would be more effective in response to the person who "treats everyone the same" and thinks that their work is done?

Example one: Equality means everyone is getting the same things or being treated the same, but this will create fairness only if everyone has started in the same place and has the same needs. Equity is about giving individuals what they need to succeed or to live happily.

Example two: Equality is handing every soldier a pair of size 10 boots. Equity is handing every soldier a pair of boots that fits their feet.

Your instinct may be to share dictionary definitions of concepts, but concrete examples that people can grasp and understand are often the truest tools for education.

Personal stories that demonstrate concepts can be even more powerful. What follows is a personal experience I like to share when I explain equality versus equity within an LGBTQ+ framework. When I go into a medical office, I get handed a form to fill out, just like everyone else (equality). As a straight, cisgender, married, monogamous woman, I typically breeze through that form without any issues. Basically, I am the soldier with the size 10 feet. If I am a lesbian trans woman in a polyamorous relationship, that form is unlikely to fit for me. I won't see myself represented with the very limited "M or F" box. I won't be sure how to respond. I will wonder if the form is asking for my biological sex or my gender. Either way this medical office will not be getting a complete picture of who I am. I am also unlikely to see my relationship status represented with the usual boxes of Married, Single, Divorced, and Separated. This medical facility is treating everyone the same by handing them the same form, but the form doesn't actually fit for lots of people. When we look hard at what "treating everyone the same" means, we often discover that it means that we are treating everyone as if they were white, straight, cisgender, monogamous, hearing, able-bodied, and middle to upper class.

The second way an ally can approach this topic with someone who feels good about treating everyone the same is to help the person understand that individuals have different identities, beliefs, abilities, experiences, and needs, and they don't necessarily *want* to be treated the same as everyone else. The way I make this concept personal is to offer examples of how I treat my friends when they come over for dinner. When Mike comes over I make sure there are nut-free food options, since he has a nut allergy. When Todd comes over I try and keep the number of guests small, because he is Deaf and it's very hard for him to follow the conversation in large groups. When Owen and Sara come over with their little boys, I put out toys. And when Pam comes over I make darn sure the whiskey bottle is full. I *never* treat my friends the same. Different behaviors on my part make their time at my house much more enjoyable.

WHY DO LGBTQ+ PEOPLE HAVE TO FLAUNT THEIR SEXUALITY AND GET IN MY FACE WITH IT?

My approach to answering this question typically starts by assessing what the asker means by the word *flaunt*. I can think of two reasons why someone might think an LGBTQ+ person was flaunting their sexuality, and my reply will depend on the asker's response. If, in fact, the person is actually full-on flaunting their identity or identities, I think back to Vivienne Cass's identity pride stage, discussed in chapter 3. Remember how in that stage, the LGBTQ+ individual is finally out and authentic and it feels *so* frickin' good? This is the stage where a person might actually be a bit "in your face"—and, in my humble opinion, they deserve it! They have had to hide who they are for so long and it feels fantastic to be out.

The savvy ally can help others understand why this individual might be super enthusiastic about their LGBTQ+ identity and excited about announcing it to the world. Personal examples can be very helpful here too. You might say something like, "I can't even imagine what it would be like to have to hide who I was or feel shame about my identity. What would that even be like, to have to constantly lie about who you live with and what you did over the weekend? It would be difficult to believe that there was nothing wrong with me. If and when I finally had the courage to break free from all of that, and live authentically, holy cow! I'd be throwing rainbow confetti in *everyone's* faces! I think if we're patient and supportive, [fill in name of flaunty friend] will settle down. But for now, let's just be happy for them and let them celebrate."

Sometimes it may seem as if a person is "flaunting" or "in your face" with their identity, but in fact they are doing no such thing. The offended person may simply have a double standard. My friend and mentor Scott (to whom I have dedicated this book) tells a story about when he moved from rural Minnesota to northern New Jersey. Suddenly everyone seemed to be "in his face" with their Jewish faith. He says that his "ears were bent out of shape" because he was hearing all these new words (like gefilte fish) and new holidays (like Rosh Hashanah) and it felt like people were inappropriately flaunting their faith and beliefs. With time, he realized that these folks were doing nothing different from what the folks back in his hometown did when they talked about Christmas, Easter, and potlucks at their local church. His ears were simply not used to hearing these new terms.

Let's say a coworker asks a colleague what she did over the weekend and she responds, "My girlfriend and I went to a *Star Trek* convention." The coworker may be thinking, "Yeesh! All I did was try and make polite conversation and she has to go and throw her sexual orientation in my face." However, if the colleague had said, "My boyfriend and I went to a *Star Trek* convention," this coworker would very likely have moved past this comment and onto bigger and better things, like offering up the Vulcan salute. This woman is not flaunting her sexuality by answering the question the way she did. She is simply being authentic in the workplace and refusing to lie or switch pronouns for a coworker's comfort.

I *KNOW* MY FRIEND IS GAY—HOW CAN I GET HIM TO COME OUT TO ME?

You can't. No one can or should drag anyone kicking and screaming out of the closet. What you *can* do, however, is create safe and inclusive spaces with your language and your actions that make it clear to your friend that if they do come out you will support them 100 percent. Here are some ways that you can do that:

- Always use inclusive and ungendered language when speaking and writing, for example, "Are you seeing anyone special?" rather than "Do you have a girlfriend?"
- Get "caught" watching or reading something that's so gay (in that real way)! Subscribe to an LGBTQ+ magazine or publication and leave it on your coffee table when you're done reading it. Read books with LGBTQ+ themes and keep them on your bookshelf in a highly visible area. Suggest a movie with LGBTQ+ themes the next time you go out.
- Express your opinion when LGBTQ+ topics come up. This can be as simple as saying something like, "I really feel like we need to do a better job making this country safe and inclusive for LGBTQ+ people. There's still a lot of work to be done."
- Wear an "I'm an ally" pin or tee shirt with a big, fat rainbow on it![4]

All four of these tips are wonderful ways for us to stay up to date on LGBTQ+ culture and language and show the world that we are welcoming and inclusive, so do them all the time. Don't implement them only when your one particular friend who you think might be gay is around. And keep in mind that you may be wrong about your friend. Remember, gaydar is unreliable. But you're an ally! Go ahead and flaunt it! Maybe your "gay" friend—who, as it turns out, isn't really gay—will become an active ally too!

WHY ISN'T THERE A STRAIGHT PRIDE PARADE?

This topic is so very important for allies to understand and know how to address. It can present itself in a variety of ways. People have asked:

"Where's *my* special safe space?"
"Why are LGBTQ+ people such special snowflakes?"
"Why should LGBTQ+ people get special rights?"

The sentiment behind all of these questions is pretty much the same. Why are we focusing on one group of overly sensitive people? What makes them more important than the rest of us?

Here are just a few of the many realities of living life as an LGBTQ+ person. These reality checks may help people understand why the LGBTQ+ population may have a greater need than the general public for identified safe spaces or a loud and proud Pride parade.

Reality Check #1

"Straight Pride" happens every day. What I mean by that is straight and cisgender people see ourselves represented constantly. I have never doubted that straight/cisgender people have invented cool stuff, created awesome art, built tall buildings, and won Pulitzer Prizes. An LGBTQ+ child working their way through the average K–12 school system might get the impression that no LGBTQ+ person has ever done anything of consequence or contributed anything to our society. LGBTQ+ people in general do not see themselves represented in our school curricula. It's still difficult to find good, positive representations of LGBTQ+ individuals in mainstream media, films, news, or books. Once a year, at Pride—if a person is lucky enough to live in a city where it's celebrated—LGBTQ+ individuals get to see people like themselves being out and proud and celebrating their existence. Cheers to that!

Reality Check #2

I received my master's degree in social work in 1992. I found it interesting that, in my diversity course, LGBTQ+ individuals were never discussed. But hey—that was 1992. Well, guess what? A few years ago, when I was facilitating a workshop in California, a young woman in my session had just finished her master's degree in social work, and she told me that the same was true for her!

Diversity in her 2016 social work master's program meant race, ethnicity, ability, class, and religion, but not LGBTQ+ identities. Even in diversity and inclusion conversations, LGBTQ+ people are often left out. Therefore, general statements like, "We do not discriminate," or, "Everyone is welcome here," might actually come with a subtext: "except for you LGBTQ+ people." When LGBTQ+ individuals walk into a health clinic, counseling center, school, recreation center, or shop, they are looking for more than general diversity statements. They are looking for safe zone or safe space stickers, LGBTQ+ images on the walls, LGBTQ+ magazines in the waiting area, and visible nondiscrimination statements and policies that specifically mention LGBTQ+ people. They can't otherwise be certain that general promises to value diversity really apply to them. LGBTQ+ people are looking for rainbows.

Reality Check #3

LGBTQ+ people are not seeking special rights; they are seeking human rights that others already have. Discrimination is very real, and unfortunately it is still legal in many states and in many countries. Fighting for legal protections people don't have doesn't make them "special snowflakes." It also doesn't make someone like me, with my legal rights fully in place, less important—and it doesn't threaten my rights.

Reality Check #4

When a child or teenager is bullied at school for being different, in most cases they can seek comfort and support at home. If the bullying is about race, religion, or ethnicity, their parents may have experienced the same kind of bullying when they were in school, and they may have some helpful suggestions for their child on how to deal with it. But with LGBTQ+ children and teens, parents can sometimes be the main source of the stress and harm. LGBTQ+ children and teens are often in a unique situation where they truly feel like they have no one to turn to. As I mentioned earlier, the suicide and attempted suicide rates for LGBTQ+ individuals, especially for transgender people, are significantly higher than those for straight and cisgender people. Having identified safe people and places for LGBTQ+ people literally saves lives.

WHY ARE LGBTQ+ PEOPLE SO ANGRY?

LGBTQ+ people are often accused of being angry and aggressive. Invariably, my tactic for educating on this topic involves putting ourselves in someone else's shoes, so to speak, but understanding the situation or incident that prompted the question gives me a concrete example to work with.

If a person is simply making a general comment about a trend that they have noticed about LGBTQ+ people, I explain the identity pride stage. As allies we should help people understand why an LGBTQ+ person who has had to hide who they are for so long might have some anger when they finally are able to live authentically. You know I am a fan of helping people grasp concepts by using personal stories. The one I like to use in this situation is to compare what I worried about in high school with what my LGBTQ+ friends worried about in high school. My LGBTQ+ high school friends, all closeted at the time, were agonizing over questions like: What is wrong with me? What if someone finds out? Am I the only one like this? I, on the other hand, was worrying about whether or not I was going to have a pimple on my nose on prom night. If I had spent years and years of my life hiding and hating a part of myself because of societal pressures, I would be angry too. Being closeted damages the soul. An angry or aggressive demeanor may stem from a "don't *ever* tell me to go back in the closet again" attitude.

If the question is prompted by a specific incident, then I work with that. A few examples of these incidents might be:

"I accidentally used the wrong pronoun for my coworker and she went apeshit on me!"

"I always try and help my single coworker find a nice girl. Today, when I tried to set him up with my neighbor, he yelled at me, 'I'm gay! Okay?'"

"I met a really awesome woman at a bar last night. She told me that she was bisexual. I told her I thought that was super hot. She told me I was an asshole."

These are all examples of microaggressions. The term *microaggresion* was originally used by and is credited to Harvard University professor Chester M. Pierce.[5] Microaggressions are commonplace comments or behaviors that are hurtful, insulting, or demeaning. They may be intentional or unintentional. In the situations I have just shared, none of these comments were meant to be demeaning or hurtful. In fact, the second situation, trying to set up a coworker with a date, is clearly meant very kindly. This makes it even harder for people to understand when they receive an angry response. As allies we can acknowledge their kind intent, but our goal should be to help people understand the impact of their words.

My friend Maur once shared with me that repeated microaggressions are like having someone flick you in the arm over and over.

Flick-Flick-Flick. The first few times you're all, "Whatever. I'm sure they didn't mean it."

Flick-Flick-Flick. Then you start to get a bit irritated.

Flick-Flick-Flick. Eventually, you get snippy with the flicker.

Flick-Flick-Flick. Finally you can't stand it anymore, and you explode.

Let's say a trans man has just had a long day at work, where he was repeatedly called "she" and "her." On his way home he stops for some milk at the grocery store and the cashier says, "Have a nice day, Ma'am." That cashier may have just administered that final "flick." The trans man explodes and the cashier is left thinking, "Wow! What the hell did I do?" or, if the trans man stuck around long enough to explain why he was so annoyed, the cashier may be left thinking, "Golly. Transgender people are *so* angry!"

LGBTQ+ people have a right to be angry when they are repeatedly marginalized by people. Allies are frequently in a better position to step in and handle the emotional labor of helping people understand the impact of their words and behaviors. The "switch it" technique can be useful here as a tool. Ask the person who is struggling to understand this anger to think about how they might feel if their coworkers constantly called them by the wrong name and pronoun or repeatedly tried to fix them up with a nice guy (if they're a straight man) or nice gal (if they're a straight woman).

A final note on "angry" or "aggressive" LGBTQ+ people goes back to our conversation on intersectionality. In our society, the people who are perceived as or accused of being angry and aggressive are *much* more likely to be women and people of color. Therefore, there is often a heightened sensitivity around this comment in these populations—and rightfully so. White, straight, cisgender men are allowed, and in many ways encouraged, to experience and show anger and aggression. Women and people of color are not. As allies we need to be aware of these double standards and stereotypes and work to combat them.

MY LESBIAN FRIENDS CALL EACH OTHER DYKES. WHY IS IT OKAY FOR THEM TO DO THAT BUT NOT ME?

Within marginalized communities it's not uncommon for people to reclaim or joke around with words that have been or still are being used against them. It's a way to disarm the people who are using derogatory terms and to take back control of an ugly situation. We have seen this with the word *queer*, which we discussed in chapter 2. However, unlike the word *queer*, which has become fairly mainstream, there are some hurtful words that are truly off-limits for folks not in the community.

My friends Gloria and Susan, a lesbian couple, were once sitting in Boston traffic, and they noticed two women in the car next to them. Gloria said to Susan, "I bet that's a couple of dykes on their way to Provincetown." They got a closer look and realized that it was their friends. Gloria then exclaimed, "Hey! It *is* a couple of dykes on their way to Provincetown!"

Because they told me this story, I might think that it's okay to use the word *dyke* to refer to my friends Gloria and Susan, because they used it. It's not. I might also think that because they shared this story with me, I am "in the club," so to speak, so that definitely makes it okay for me to use the term. It doesn't.

I have never had the word *dyke* used against me. It's not my word to reclaim or neutralize. Rather than feel hurt that I am not allowed to use reclaimed terms, I should feel honored when my LGBTQ+ friends feel comfortable and safe enough around me to use them in my presence and trust me not to misuse them. Using a reclaimed derogatory term will not prove to anyone that I am "in the club"; it will just piss people off.

If you're not sure what's okay and what's off limits, simply ask: "Hey, I heard you use the term _____ earlier tonight. I want to make sure that I am being respectful. Is that an okay term for me to use too, or should I avoid it?"

I THOUGHT PEOPLE WERE "BORN THAT WAY"; NOW YOU'RE TELLING ME THAT THIS CAN BE A LIFELONG JOURNEY OF CHANGING IDENTITIES? WTF?

People cannot choose their gender identity or control whom they are attracted to. If we could, then conversion therapy (i.e., "counseling away the gay") would actually work, which it doesn't. Conversion therapy has occasionally been able to shame or scare a person into temporarily altering their behavior, but it has never been able to change someone's orientation.[6]

So, if we cannot control our gender identity or our orientation, what's up with folks who identified as straight for twenty-five years, then gay for ten years, and are now bisexual? (This totally happens.) Or, as we talked about in chapter 3, what about people who first identified as cisgender lesbians and now identify as straight transgender men? (This also totally happens.)

We cannot control our gender identity or whom we are attracted to, but our understanding and our acceptance of who we are can take lots of different twists, turns, and paths and can be an extremely long journey for many people. Some people, like my friend Dee in chapter 2, struggle to find their identity word and may initially use words that don't quite fit. My friend Kayden, a trans man who once identified as a lesbian, says, "It's like when you go to the mall, and you fill up at the food court, and then go and try on jeans. You try them on and they kind of fit but are difficult to button. That's what the term *lesbian* felt like for me."

Others may live in geographical areas where they are not exposed to the people or the communities that would help them identify their terms. Over time, as people move through the world, meet new people, and hear new terms (Hurray for new terms!), they may have an "aha!" moment—or several "aha!" moments—with new identity terms that work better for them. My friend Jason, editor in chief at *FTM Magazine*, told me that finding his identity words, *straight trans* man, felt like slipping his feet into his girlfriend's soft, fuzzy UGGs.

Still others may suppress or reject their identities for long periods of time, fearful of the consequences of living as their authentic selves. I know many individuals who consciously waited until their parents died before coming out and living authentically because they didn't want to deal with the trauma and shame they suspected would have been their reality if their parents knew their true identity.

POP QUIZ

You work at a senior living facility and one of your residents comes out as a transgender woman. You should: (Choose all that apply)

A. Congratulate her on being brave and authentic!
B. Show your support by buying her some handbags and lipstick.
C. Show your support by asking her what name and pronoun you should now use for her and asking her when and where it's okay to use them.
D. Show your support by asking her how you can help her with her journey.

Answer: A, C, and D

Interestingly, the staff member at the senior living facility who called me and asked for my advice very kindly—but inappropriately—went for answer B. Handbags and lipstick may have been welcomed and appreciated by this woman, but they also may not have been. Everyone's gender expression is unique and personal. It would have been best to find out first if this woman wanted any assistance or advice regarding her wardrobe or cosmetics, rather than assuming.

A resident in her early eighties residing at a senior living facility in Upstate New York recently came out as transgender. From the outside world looking in, people see an eighty-year-old who has suddenly "become transgender"—so weird! But the reality is that she had been struggling her entire life with her identity as a transgender woman. When she saw Laverne Cox and Caitlyn Jenner on television and in magazines, she finally said to herself, "What the heck am I waiting for?"

One final note on this topic, many people who are confused by other people's changing identities may actually be confusing attraction and behavior, as discussed in chapter 4. If this is the case, the question may sound something like this: "My niece came out as bisexual three years ago. Now she just announced that she's getting married to a guy. Did she turn straight?" Clearly the asker is confusing the niece's attraction/orientation with her behaviors/relationship choices. Try the "switch it" technique to help this person understand the difference: for example, if a straight woman gets a divorce from her husband and is currently not in a relationship with anyone, does that mean she's not straight anymore? The answer is: Of course not.

I FEEL LIKE I CAN'T SAY ANYTHING ANYMORE WITHOUT OFFENDING SOMEONE. DON'T YOU THINK WE'VE GONE TOO FAR WITH ALL OF THIS PC LANGUAGE?

I remember the first time a workshop participant suggested that I remove the word *preferred* from my question when I asked people if they would like to share their preferred pronouns. Did I immediately take that new piece of information, stick it into my lump of knowledge, and change my behavior? Nope. I thought about it for a moment and then dismissed it with a "nah."

As an educator, I think back to that moment often, not because I am proud of it—obviously I'm not—but because it's truly fascinating to me. There I was, facilitating a workshop focused on being mindful of language and making respectful word choices, and suddenly—*bam!*—I'm the learner, and a resistant one at that.

As you know, I now encourage people to remove the word *preferred* when they ask people to share their pronouns. So what happened? What made me change my mind? What was the process? Well, first I began to hear a few other folks also recommend this language tweak. (Yes. I think that sometimes numbers *do* matter. I have had individuals from marginalized communities suggest that I change my language, only to find out later that this was a personal choice that the majority of the other members from that community didn't agree with. In these cases I do my best to remember that language tweak when I am speaking with the individual, but I don't make that change in my workshops or daily life.) Then I did a little research into whether or not this was becoming "a thing." (That may sound odd, but some new trends take hold and become "things" while others disappear within months.) Finally, I applied the "switch it" technique and realized that, in fact, we *don't* ask cisgender people about their *preferred* pronouns. It was clearly a logical request. So I changed my language.

The beauty of realizing that I am fully capable of experiencing that "Really? Now I'm being asked to change this too?" reaction is that when someone asks me this question about PC (politically correct) language, I understand where they're coming from. We have common ground. I demonstrate this to them by using a connecting statement like, "I get it. I have felt that way too." If you can't find common ground with the person because you have never felt this way yourself, try connecting with them by letting them know you think it's unfortunate that they feel they can no longer have conversations with people.

People should be having conversations, and this topic in particular is a great one for allies to take the lead on. Allies are in a better position to offer safe, non-judgmental spaces for people to talk through their frustration with language than are community members who are directly impacted by people's word choices. Commiserate, connect if you can, allow people to share their annoyance, and then offer pointers. Here are three major language stumbling blocks that can prevent people from changing their language and some tips for helping folks get over them:

- *Not Fully Understanding the Point:* As we discussed in chapter 2, when people already have their identity words, whether they are a part of the LGBTQ+ communities or not, it's more difficult for them to understand the need for new ones. Use a personal example involving the positive impact of someone using correct and respectful language, if you have one. If you don't, consider sharing the story about Dee finding her identity word or Kayden forcing those jeans on after hitting the food court. You can also share the article by Alex Myers (referenced in chapter 2) about why we need more LGBTQ+ labels and identities, not fewer. Finally, if applicable, try the "switch it" technique. It worked well in helping me see the logic behind changing my language with *preferred* pronouns.
- *Disliking Being Told What to Do:* No one likes being told what they have to do. If people are feeling pressured or forced into changing something by the "PC police"—especially if that change doesn't make sense to them— they are very likely to feel frustration, anger, and resistance. One way to

help is to ask them to change what PC stands for in their heads. Instead of "politically correct," ask them to think about PC as standing for "please consider." *They* get to choose whether or not they change their language. Tell them to stop worrying about whether or not the "PC police" are going to slap them with a ticket, and instead put their energy into thinking about *why* they are being asked to change their language. If it makes sense to them, then they should make the change. If it doesn't, they shouldn't. But do encourage them to make an informed decision and to be open to altering their choice with time. Ask them to think about some words they used as a child that they now consider offensive; this should help them see that they have been making word choices and being intentional in their language their whole lives.

- *Feeling Overwhelmed:* Even *I* sometimes get overwhelmed with all the language changes and updates that take place within the LGBTQ+ communities, and I run workshops on LGBTQ+ inclusion! It is no surprise that people who don't have a strong connection to the LGBTQ+ communities also feel overwhelmed. Trying to learn all of the newest terms and remembering to replace them with the ones we have been using our whole lives can feel like a daunting task. One of the suggestions I like to offer people comes from my experience learning how to play racquetball. Having never played the game before, I started playing weekly with a friend who knew the game well. Each week I got my ass thoroughly kicked. I was completely overwhelmed by how many things there were to think about during the game, and I did none of them well. After about six weeks of this nonsense, I'd had enough. I decided I would focus on one skill every time we played. I would forgive myself for everything else I messed up on and just focus on doing that one thing well. It worked like a charm. My skills increased and my frustration dissipated rapidly. If people are feeling overwhelmed with all the language changes they are being asked to make, encourage them to focus on just one. Ask them to choose one word or language tweak that is important to them or that makes sense to them and just work on that until they have it down. Then they can move on to another.

It can be difficult to change our word choices, but typically people are willing to put in the work if the concept makes sense to them, if they are not feeling forced, and if they can keep from feeling completely overwhelmed in the process. With a little savvy ally encouragement, you can help people enjoy the satisfaction of being intentional in their language as a way of supporting other people in living their lives authentically and proudly.

NOTES

1. Human Rights Campaign, "State Maps of Laws & Policies," https://www.hrc.org/state-maps/.

2. Ibid.

3. *Wikipedia*, "LGBT Rights by Country or Territory," https://en.wikipedia.org/wiki/LGBT_rights_by_country_or_territory.

4. These suggestions have been adapted from the Out Alliance handout "Is My Child LGBTQ+?"

5. *Wikipedia*, "Microaggression," https://en.wikipedia.org/wiki/Microaggression.

6. "The Lies and Dangers of Efforts to Change Sexual Orientation or Gender Identity," Human Rights Campaign, accessed October 21, 2019, https://www.hrc.org/resources/the-lies-and-dangers-of-reparative-therapy.

DUCT TAPE PATCH-UP JOBS AND BIG FIXES

Two Paths to Travel toward More Inclusive Spaces

When you come to a fork in the road, take it!

—Yogi Berra

Let's imagine that my friend Shimona comes over to my house for dinner. On her way to my door she trips on an uneven section of my front walk. She falls, rips her pants, and gets a big gash on her knee. Ouch!

I, of course, feel terrible. I apologize, I get her what she needs to clean the wound, and we bandage her knee. I have just offered a "duct tape patch-up job" solution to the situation: in this case, a sincere apology, some antiseptic, and a bandage. A lesser response would have been exhibiting extremely rude behavior: "Oh bummer, Shimona. That knee is a bloody mess. Can you please bleed on the kitchen tile instead of the rug?"

But the problem remains. I still have an uneven walkway. If I don't also come up with a "big fix" solution by repairing my front walkway, then next week, when my friend Manuel comes over for dinner, he is likely to trip as well. Even worse, a few months later, Shimona may come back and trip on the very same spot again! How embarrassing! By offering Shimona an apology and some first aid I have offered temporary care, but I have not actually fixed the problem. I must travel down both of these paths, the short-term fix and the big-picture fix, in order to create a safe and welcoming space for my visitors. We must do the same at our schools, agencies, businesses, and faith communities in order to create safe, welcoming, and inclusive spaces for LGBTQ+ people.

Imagine that a nonbinary person named Bo comes in for care at a mental health center. The form Bo is given has an "M or F" box option, most of the staff members are unfamiliar with nonbinary identities, and there are only "men's" and "women's" restrooms. This center has a client who currently doesn't fit into its system or its space. The immediate care that must be given is the duct tape patch-up job, which should probably involve a sincere apology, extra privacy for sensitive conversations, and creative temporary fixes like an "all-gender restroom" sign stuck on one of the bathroom doors with tape. This center is not an inclusive space yet, but some efforts have been made to help Bo feel welcome.

When Bo leaves, there is more work to be done. The staff should now think about the big fixes that need to happen. In this case some long-term changes that need to take place are building renovations (including the creation of some all-gender restrooms), mandatory and ongoing staff trainings on LGBTQ+ identities, and updated database categories, policies, and forms.

What follows are some key areas where allies can work to create safer, more welcoming, and more inclusive spaces. I have offered both duct tape patch-up job suggestions and big-fix solutions for each area. Allies should travel down both paths whenever possible and advocate for others to do so as well.[1]

EDUCATIONAL OPPORTUNITIES

Much of this book is focused on taking advantage of educational opportunities when they arise. Speaking up when we hear something offensive and creating safe and judgment-free spaces for having respectful conversations with people are huge parts of an ally's role. In earlier chapters I offered some tools allies can use to do this effectively. In this section we will look at when and where those respectful conversations can be used for both short- and long-term solutions.

Duct tape patch-up job educational efforts are immediate reactions to comments or behaviors that are not okay. These educational opportunities can spring up anywhere: at work, with a neighbor, with our kids, with teammates, or at school. Big fix educational efforts change the environment in our workplaces, neighborhoods, homes, and schools, making them safer and more inclusive.

Let's take a look at educational opportunities in schools. In most K–12 schools in the United States, duct tape patch-up jobs are the *only* actions taking place. Most schools believe that if they are either not seeing bullying of LGBTQ+ people or are already dealing with the bullying, then they have created an inclusive environment. They haven't. They are simply snuffing out a negative behavior. The underlying issue is still there. In his book *Safe Is Not Enough: Better Schools for LGBTQ Students*, Michael Sadowski asks, "Is safety the only thing to which LGBTQ students are entitled at school?"[2] Let's hope not.

My friend Matt grew up in an Upstate New York suburb and attended the public school there. From kindergarten until about tenth grade, he never heard the word *gay* spoken in a positive way by anyone—students, teachers, school staff, or administrators. As a young man figuring out his identity as a cisgender gay man, he said that he didn't experience much name-calling or bullying; there was just this resounding silence when it came to anything LGBTQ+ related. It wasn't until tenth-grade health class that he finally heard the word *gay* spoken by a teacher—and guess what they were talking about? AIDS and HIV. The very first time Matt heard his identity spoken by a teacher, it had to do with disease and death. Matt said this made him want no part of being gay. He sat in that stage of identity tolerance for years and years instead of moving forward and being able to live authentically. And yet the school's administrators and teachers probably thought their school was really inclusive because there was little to no bullying of LGBTQ+ students.

Matt shared with me that if one teacher in elementary school had added a word problem in math class that said: "Peter invited 12 kids to his birthday party. His two moms bought 3 pizzas with 8 slices each . . ." his mind would have been blown! He told me that seeing a gay couple normalized in this way in the school curriculum would have sent him down a much healthier path toward self-acceptance.

My children, along with most kids in the United States, have known how to stop, drop, and roll since kindergarten. They were taught and retaught this fire safety technique throughout their K–12 school experience. I am truly thankful. However, I once looked into the likelihood of a child dying in a house fire in the United States: It is about 1 in 90,000. What are the chances that that child will discover at some point in their life that they are LGBTQ+? The estimates are about 1 in 20. Yet our schools remain mostly silent on the subject. Without LGBTQ+ teachers as role models, LGBTQ+ historical figures included in the curriculum, and any positive LGBTQ+ characters in textbooks or literature, these children are left to cope with understanding and accepting their identities completely on their own. Parents are left unsupported, not knowing how to react when their children come out to them or how to support them. Schools' silence about LGBTQ+ people sends a very loud and clear message.

Duct Tape Patch-Up Jobs with Our Educational Opportunities

- Speak up when a teammate refers to an opponent with a derogatory term.
- Offer a workplace or school diversity training as a reaction to an incident or concern.
- Respond to your child's question, "What does gay mean?"
- Send a child who is bullying another child to the principal's office, where the bullying will be dealt with appropriately.

Big Fixes with Our Educational Opportunities

- Make ongoing, mandatory LGBTQ+ workshops a part of your workplace or school diversity and inclusion efforts.
- Incorporate LGBTQ+ awareness and inclusion into all new staff orientations and trainings.
- Include LGBTQ+ individuals and families into everyday school curricula (e.g., math, English, history, and science), not just health class.
- From a very early age, read books to your child that have all kinds of people and families in them, and where all types of gender roles and expressions are represented.

HELPFUL HINT

Some of my favorite picture books for young children with LGBTQ+ themes are:

Red: A Crayon's Story, by Michael Hall: A charming book about the importance of living authentically, even if your exterior doesn't match your interior. This beautifully illustrated book follows the story of a crayon that is labeled "red" but can only color in blue.

King and King, by Linda De Haan: This is the story of young Prince Bertie, whose mother is trying to get him to marry a nice princess. None of the princesses catch Prince Bertie's eye, but it's love at first sight when he sees Prince Lee! The story ends with a happy and drama-free prince-and-prince wedding.

Families, Families, Families! by Suzanne Lang: Cartoon animals represent all kinds of families in this simple picture book. The child who has two mommies will see their family represented in this book. So will the child being raised by a single parent or by Grandma. This book helps children understand what makes a family. Surprise—it's love!

VISIBLE LGBTQ+ IMAGES

I mentioned in chapter 9 that LGBTQ+ people are typically looking for more than a general sign stating that an agency or shop does not discriminate. This means we have an opportunity as allies to help LGBTQ+ people feel safe and welcome by queering up our spaces! Think about whether or not LGBTQ+ individuals walking into your shop, agency, school, health center, office space, faith community, or home see themselves represented and welcomed.

Several years ago, a young cisgender gay man at a workshop I offered in the Philadelphia area told the group a powerful story. As a college student in an area of the United States not well known for its LGBTQ+ inclusion, he was alone and unsupported, was just barely tolerating himself as a gay man, and was contemplating suicide. During his junior year, two rainbow safe space stickers popped up on office doors in one of the buildings where he attended classes. He told us that he would wait until it was late in the evening and he knew that no one would be around, and then he would return to that hallway where the stickers were and walk up and down to "gather strength" from them. The fact that there were two professors on his campus who thought that being gay was okay gave him an incredible amount of hope. He said that those stickers kept him alive. This young gay man never had the courage to actually walk through the door into those offices, so those two professors to this day have no idea that they saved a man's life.

When we offer visible support for the LGBTQ+ communities, we will be aware of the LGBTQ+ folks who come in and chat about their identities or thank us for our support. However, our visible support of LGBTQ+ people will have the biggest impact on the ones who can't walk through our door. Being visibly LGBTQ+ inclusive and supportive saves lives.

Duct Tape Patch-Up Jobs with Our Visible LGBTQ+ Images

- Add an LGBTQ+ magazine or newspaper to your waiting area.
- Tape up a sign with a rainbow that says, "All families welcome here."
- Fly a rainbow flag outside your workplace, home, or place of worship.
- Wear or attach an ally or rainbow pin, zipper pull, or bag tag.

Big Fixes with our LGBTQ+ Images

- Subscribe to an LGBTQ+ magazine or newspaper for your waiting area.
- Create permanent images of LGBTQ+ people and statements of inclusion for your walls and website.

- Update promotional materials (e.g., posters and pamphlets) to include images of all different types of families.
- Recognize LGBT Pride Month in June every year by creating a Pride display.

A HELPFUL HINT ABOUT SAFE SPACES

Anyone can put up a sign with a rainbow image that says, "All families welcome here." However, safe space (sometimes called safe zone) stickers and signs imply more. Safe space stickers and signs are typically offered after a safe space workshop, and they indicate that the person displaying them has had some training about LGBTQ+ identities and inclusion. Safe space images are well known within the LGBTQ+ communities and are hugely impactful. They indicate to LGBTQ+ people where they can go if they need to talk with someone, need resources, or just need to be in a space where they can be authentic. If you are interested in being trained, check with the college campus or LGBTQ+ center nearest you to see if they offer these workshops. Also check out the Safe Zone trainings and other great workshops at the Out Alliance (https://outalliance.org/) and Acronym Project (https://theacronymproject.com/).

FORMS AND PAPERWORK

Unless you live under a rock, you are likely to often find yourself filling out paper and online forms. We encounter them in copious amounts from schools, insurance companies, healthcare facilities, and employers. We have to fill them out when we purchase airline tickets, join an athletic club, and shop online. They are everywhere.

My identities and relationship are fully recognized by our society and on all forms. I can walk into a doctor's office and check off the "F" box for my sex and gender. (These two identities are often confused and combined on forms, but it doesn't matter for me, since my sex and gender align.) Then I check off "Married" under the heading "Relationship Status." If it's an OB/GYN office or breast care center, most likely the questions will all be written with the assumption that I was assigned female at birth, that I identify as a woman, that I have one sexual partner, and that my partner is a man. Before I worked for an LGBTQ+ center I would fill out these forms and not think twice about them or even notice that the questions were extremely narrow and limiting.

What is this medical visit going to look like if I am intersex? Bisexual? Polyamorous? Transgender? Possibly patients with these identities will be disconcerted by the form and the fact that their identities are not represented there. They may fear that the staff will not be respectful, educated, and open to their identities. Some may leave without ever seeing the doctor. Others will fudge their way through the form, leaving some things blank or creating new boxes, then mentally prepare themselves for what is likely to be several awkward conversations with the medical staff—like my friend Dee, a transgender woman, who had this awkward conversation in a not-so-private area at her doctor's office:

Medical Staff Member: When was your last menstrual period?

Dee: Um.

Medical Staff Member: Was it within the past six weeks?

Dee: Well . . .

Medical Staff Member: You don't remember?

Dee: Not really.

Medical Staff Member: Are you irregular?

Dee: Yes. I'm irregular.

One of the first things patients are asked to do upon entering a medical facility is fill out a form. What a wonderful opportunity to show immediately that your agency is welcoming and inclusive. Rather than cause stress, medical professionals can welcome patients with a form that acknowledges everyone and all types of relationships. A bonus of having more inclusive forms is that it helps prevent situations like the one Dee encountered. If the staff member takes the form from Dee and sees that Dee is a transgender woman, she is unlikely to ask openly, where other patients can hear her, when Dee's last menstrual period took place.

I view noninclusive forms as a perfect opportunity to step in with savvy ally action! Why should we leave this educational opportunity to the folks who likely are already feeling extremely stressed and vulnerable? As a straight cisgender ally, I am at extremely low risk for any negative consequences if I advocate for more inclusive forms, so I am the perfect person to do it.

Typically what I do when I am given a noninclusive form is offer some suggestions on the side of the page, like: "Please consider asking this question in a different way to be more LGBTQ+ inclusive. Feel free to contact me if you would like some suggestions." (Yup, I really do this.) Usually my "helpful" comment gets ignored, but I have possibly planted a seed. If a dozen clients comment similarly on their noninclusive form, the staff are likely to take action.

Every once in a while good things happen and I am asked to offer assistance. Here is an example of a time when a good thing happened. Several years back, the intake form at my OB/GYN office had this section below:

Marital Status (Circle):   S   M   Sep   D   W

I made my usual offer to help and heard nothing back. But at my annual exam the next year, I noticed the form had changed and the section now read:

Marital Status (Circle):   S   M   Sep   D   W   Female Partner

This was a "tack it on" or duct tape effort—better than making the assumption that every woman they see is straight, but marginally. Here's why:

- It makes "male partner" the norm or default. In other words, if I am married to a woman, I circle "M" and "Female Partner." If I am married to a man, I circle only "M." "Male Partner" is assumed. This is very othering. Because there is no "Male Partner" option, it's pretty clear that if you circle "Female Partner" you are different from most.
- It lumps together relationships and intimate behaviors, which may be different. For example: What do I circle if I am a woman who is married to a man but who also has a female sexual partner? If I circle "M" and "Female Partner," then the assumption will be that I am married to a woman.
- It only scratches the surface of the information the providers actually need and should know about their patients. If I circle "Female Partner" the assumption is likely to be, "This patient is a lesbian. She has one partner and the partner is a woman." The reality is that they have no information about my orientation (I may be bisexual), my gender (I may be a trans man), or my relationship status (just because I have a female partner doesn't mean I am in a relationship with that person).

This time, I waited until I was in the private room with my doctor. I told him that I was very pleased to see the effort his office had made on the form to be more inclusive. Then I told him that there were ways to make it even better and that I would be happy to help.

A few weeks later I received an e-mail from my doctor, with the intake form attached, asking for my help. Hurrah! In my e-mail back to my doctor I sent my suggestions for a completely revised form that fits *everyone*. Here were my suggestions for the section on relationship status (formerly "Marital Status"):

What is your current relationship(s) status? _____

What is your sexual orientation? _____

If they absolutely must have standardized, multiple-choice responses, I suggested something like this:

Relationship Status (Circle all that apply):
Single   Married   Separated   Divorced   Widowed   Partnered
Polyamorous   Monogamous   A relationship/partnership not listed here

Sexual Orientation (Circle all that apply):
Lesbian   Gay   Bisexual   Straight   Pansexual   Asexual   Queer
An orientation not listed here

If a patient circles "A relationship/partnership not listed here" or "An orientation not listed here," and the medical office is restricted by limited options on their computer's database, this should be explained to the patient in a private setting and the best option should be chosen with the patient's involvement. Although this is not ideal, it's significantly better and more respectful than stressing patients out with forms and options that don't fit at all.

I also shared with my doctor that this new form would give him some basic information that could help him discuss, in private, a patient's sexual behaviors. He should not make assumptions about what people are actually doing sexually based on their relationship status or their orientation.

If you would like to advocate for more inclusive forms but don't think you are the right person to offer suggestions, you can simply refer folks to the National LGBT Health Education Center's online guide *Focus on Forms and Policy: Creating an Inclusive Environment for LGBT Patients.*[3] Although the eight-page guide focuses on health, much of it can be used for general form "makeovers."

Duct Tape Patch-Up Jobs on Forms and Paperwork

- Tack on new options to an existing form, like "Female Partner."
- Offer all clients the option of filling out the current form one on one, with a staff member, in a private area.
- Add a statement that apologizes for the limited form. Let your clients know that you are currently in the process of updating it and welcome them to write whatever fill-ins or explanations they need on the current form.

- Include an "A gender not listed here" or "An orientation not listed here" option if the form doesn't already have this. These options are typically received better than "other."

Big Fixes on Forms and Paperwork

- Think long and hard about what you actually need to know. *Then* look at whether or not your questions are getting you there. Do you need to know someone's biological sex, or do you really want to know their gender? Is it important to know someone's sexual orientation or just what they are doing sexually in order to offer appropriate care? Do you need to know if someone is male or female, or do you really want to know how you should address them? Forms should be adapted to your organization's actual needs, and they should change and be updated over time.
- Survey your clients and ask them how your forms can be more inclusive and can represent their identities and their relationships, then use those suggestions in updating the forms.
- Have "Name" at the top of the form, and "Legal Name, if different" later or lower on the form. That way the person's correct and current name will always be the one that is used. Most forms have "Name" or "Legal Name" at the top of the form, with "Nickname" or "Preferred Name" listed later. This often creates a situation where the wrong name is used first, which can cause embarrassment and a potentially unsafe environment.
- If you are restricted to limited multiple-choice options by the databases that you are using, contact these companies and advocate for more inclusive categories. United Airlines recently added a nonbinary option to its gender selections, and Facebook now has a custom gender option where a person can fill in their gender and share their pronoun.

POLICIES

My education team members and I always found it incredibly ironic (and icky) when we entered a facility where we had previously offered LGBTQ+ workshops on creating inclusive spaces, only to find that my trans cofacilitator was misgendered, told they had to sign in with their "real" name, and forced to wear an ID badge with their old name printed on it for all to see. Often we find in schools, health facilities, corporations, and agencies that good work is being done by a small group of concerned people, but the big-picture stuff is not being touched, nor is it even on the radar.

Creating updated and inclusive policies is critical to protect people's rights and privacy and to create the foundation for your work toward more welcoming and inclusive spaces. That's step one. Step two is ensuring that employees, students, parents, clients, and members are aware of these policies. Participants in my trainings often have no idea what the policies are at their workplace or school. Once you do the work to bring your policies up to date, let people know what they are. Send an annual e-mail with your policies included, hang your nondiscrimination policy in a high-traffic area for all to see, and include your policies in displays celebrating honorary months like Black History Month, LGBT Pride Month, and Disability Awareness Month.

Duct Tape Patch-Up Jobs for Policies

- Train front desk staff in LGBTQ+ identities and respectful communication so that every effort can be made to help visitors deal with check-in procedures that are difficult for them. Ungendering welcomes, sincerely apologizing, lowering voices, and finding a private space for conversations will go a long way toward helping anyone who is made uncomfortable by your current policies.
- If legal name must be represented on all badges and e-mail addresses, allow people to attach a ribbon to the bottom of their badge that says, "Please call me _____" and allow them to add this to their e-mail signature. Allies can wear ribbons and add these messages to their e-mail signature too! This helps to normalize the behavior so it's not just the transgender employees being singled out. (A helpful hint for more on this concept is coming up.)
- Take a stand as a local chapter. In our area of Upstate New York several local Boy Scout troops took a stand against the Boy Scouts of America's decision not to allow gay men to be leaders. They showed visible support for their LGBTQ+ leaders, parents, and scouts on their websites and in their literature.
- Offer optional pronoun stickers or pins as people enter your workplace, school, or faith community building. Wear one yourself! This is a great way for allies to help create a more welcoming and safe space—plus, you're bound to have some great conversations about why you're wearing your pronoun on your shirt.

HELPFUL HINT

If people always, or almost always, use the correct pronoun when they refer to you, you are likely to find yourself having to answer these questions if you display your pronoun: "Why are you telling me your pronoun? Isn't it obvious?" What a great educational opportunity! Here are the reasons I display my pronouns on my e-mail signature and on my name badge. Feel free to use these reasons when explaining your choice to others.

- Displaying my pronoun helps normalize the activity and makes it easier for others to do so.
- Creating a culture where people routinely display their pronouns helps to avoid those embarrassing moments when you aren't sure how to refer to someone. It avoids having to single someone out.
- Violence against transgender people is a horrible reality. It may create a dangerous situation for transgender people if they are the only ones displaying their pronouns.

Displaying my pronoun demonstrates that I understand the need for trans-inclusive and safe spaces.

Big Fixes for Policies

- Ensure that equal opportunity employment statements, codes of conduct, antiharassment policies, benefits statements, and nondiscrimination policies include these three categories: Sexual Orientation, Gender Identity, and Gender Expression. Often you will find the first one, sometimes the second, and rarely the third. Here is how these three categories protect us:

  Sexual Orientation: People cannot be discriminated against because of whom they are attracted to. This protects gay men, lesbians, bisexual people, pansexual people, asexual people, and more.

  Gender Identity: People cannot be discriminated against for how they identify their gender. This mainly protects transgender individuals, including nonbinary folks.

  Gender Expression: People cannot be discriminated against for how they express their gender. This protects people from being told they need to dress in a way that's more feminine or more masculine. This category protects everyone.

- Ungender dress codes and uniforms. For example, rather than stating what men and women are allowed to wear, simply state, "Employees may wear pants, skirts, or dresses that are not ripped or frayed, but no shorts," or, "Students may not wear shirts that expose their bellies." When working with youth in schools, camps, or recreation centers, it's important to be aware that swimwear can be especially traumatizing for trans and gender-expansive youth, who may have intense feelings of distress about their bodies. Allow youth to wear any swim attire that makes them comfortable, including swim shirts.
- Ask everyone to share their pronouns and how they would like to be addressed, if they feel comfortable doing so. Add this question to forms and check-in procedures. Always have pronoun stickers or pins available as people enter your facility. Not everyone will want to participate, and that's fine, but it's incredibly welcoming for those who do.
- Create policies that are inclusive of transgender and transitioning employees/students. Ideally employers, colleges, and K–12 schools should have these guidelines and policies in place *before* they have to use them, but unfortunately, the first out transgender individual or the first transitioning person tends to be the guinea pig, paving the way for others. Policies should support all transgender people, including binary, nonbinary, transitioning, and nontransitioning individuals. One big area to address is name change policies. When someone legally changes their name, how is this handled when it comes to name tags, e-mail address, ID badges, directories, attendance lists, confidentiality, and communication? Are these policies also in place for someone who changes their name but has not gone through a legal name change? As mentioned earlier, the Human Rights Campaign is a great resource for transitioning employee guidelines, and is also a wonderful resource for creating trans-inclusive schools. (See http://www.welcomingschools.org.)

Whether or not you work for a corporation, I would recommend taking a look at the HRC's *Corporate Equality Index* for a very thorough description of what inclusive LGBTQ+ policies and practices look like.[4]

RESTROOMS AND OTHER FACILITIES

Single-stall, all-gender restrooms should be made available whenever possible. Access to gendered restrooms and locker rooms should be based on an indi-

FUN AND NOT-SO-FUN FACTS

- The bathrooms in your home are probably all-gender.
- In March 2016, North Carolina's House Bill 2 became the law. This bill stated that individuals may only use restrooms that correspond to the sex identified on their birth certificates. There was an enormous amount of backlash to this decision: musicians canceled rock concerts, the NCAA refused to allow North Carolina to host championship games, and large companies canceled their plans to build North Carolina–based facilities. It has been estimated that the state will lose more than $3.76 billion over the next dozen years as a result of this decision.[5] In March 2017 the bill was adapted, removing restroom restrictions for transgender people.[6]

  Some things are more important than a rock show and this fight against prejudice and bigotry—which is happening as I write—is one of them.

  —Bruce Springsteen, regarding his canceled concert in Greensboro, North Carolina

- In his TEDTalk "How to Talk (and Listen) to Transgender People," Jackson Bird informs us that "more US congressmen have been convicted of assaulting someone in a public restroom than trans people have been."[7]
- More Americans claim to have seen a ghost than claim they have met a trans person.[8] What does this have to do with restroom facilities? Nothing, really; I just thought it was a ridiculous fact. What it does indicate, however, is that we have all encountered transgender people and we have not necessarily known it. It's highly probable that you have already peed next to a transgender person. If you meet folks who feel that we should hire security guards to stand at restroom entrances and check driver's licenses, birth certificates, or genitals, direct them to the #WeJustNeedToPee campaign, initially started by Brae Carnes.[9] This campaign is a series of bathroom selfies taken and posted by transgender people to show how uncomfortable life would be if we forced people into restrooms according to the sex they were assigned at birth.

POP QUIZ

Who should use an all-gender restroom?

A. Transgender individuals
B. Transgender, questioning, and transitioning individuals
C. Anyone

Answer: C

Many people think of all-gender restrooms as "transgender bathrooms." Some transgender individuals will choose to use them and some won't. All-gender restrooms are there for *anyone* to use. What this means is, if my coworker is transitioning and I am uncomfortable being in the same restroom with her, *I* can go and use the single-stall all-gender restroom and have my privacy. Ta-da! All-gender restrooms and changing facilities can also be incredibly helpful for parents who don't want to be separated from their children while using public facilities and for adult care givers assisting people with disabilities.

vidual's gender identity, not the sex they were assigned at birth, the sex printed on their birth certificate, or their assumed biological sex. No one should ever be told which facility they must use.

Helping cisgender people understand that everyone should have access to safe facilities and relieving people's fears with information are great tasks for allies. Feel free to use the data I offered on facility use in chapter 6, or do your own research. The data will confirm that it is not cisgender people, but our transgender friends who are at risk in public facilities.

Duct Tape Patch-Up Jobs for Restrooms and Other Facilities

- Put "all-gender restroom" signs over existing gendered signs, if you already have single-stall restrooms at your school or workplace.
- Create a map to help people find all-gender restrooms. If all-gender restrooms are few and far between at your workplace or campus, this will help folks find them. Add it to the Diversity and Inclusion or Pride page on your organization's website.
- Allow students or employees who feel uncomfortable using the gendered restrooms access to special accommodations. For example, allow a student to use the private restroom in the nurse's office until better accommodations can be made.

Big Fixes for Restrooms and Other Facilities

- When renovating or designing new buildings, create at least one single-stall all-gender restroom on every floor.
- Create locker room facilities that have private changing areas and private showers. This is likely to make many students very happy! How many middle-school kids are comfortable putting their naked bodies on display for their peers? (That was a rhetorical question. I know the answer.)
- Offer only all-gender single-stall restrooms when feasible. Many restaurants now offer only a single all-gender restroom, a couple of all-gender restrooms, or a whole row of them. Ever see women waiting in a long line for the single-stall women's room, while the single-stall men's room sits unused? There are almost always a few rebels (myself included) who say, "This is so ridiculous," and just go ahead and use the men's room. Why are we gendering single-stall restrooms?

TOILET TALK

I have now had enough conversations with cisgender women who are against all-gender restrooms based solely on the complaint that "men pee everywhere," that I felt it merited some candid toilet talk. Let me begin by stating that, generally, if my husband, Ed, is coming out of the men's room at a gas station or restaurant shaking his head and saying, "Gross," I am coming out of the women's restroom doing the same thing. However, for argument's sake, let's say that all-gender restrooms are generally less clean than women's restrooms. What we are now weighing is inconveniencing cisgender women against keeping transgender people safe. I'll take the messy restroom any day. Perhaps our work as allies should include advocating for cleaner restrooms so that *everyone* can pee and peace out safely and without sticky shoes.

On a more positive note, I have been to many restaurants that offer a row of clean, private, all-gender restrooms, and I think they are much better than the large gendered rooms with stalls. If you're pee-shy, you can pee (or take care of other stuff) comfortably, without angst over who is listening. You get your own personal sink. And you don't have to worry about how silly you look checking your teeth for green stuff.

A Special Note about Signage

I field a lot of questions about the best sign to use for all-gender restrooms. (I've just given you a big hint.) "All-Gender Restroom" will do just fine. "Gender-Neutral Restroom" also works. Here are a few signs to avoid and the reasons why.

Woman and Man Images

 This implies that there are only two genders. It's very binary. Are nonbinary folks welcome to use that facility? What about women who are not wearing dresses? What about people with necks? (Too far?)

Family Restroom

 The implication here is that folks using this restroom should have a child or children in tow. An individual exiting a family restroom without a child is at risk for dirty looks and possibly even harassment.

Half-and-Half Person

 Please avoid the image of the person who has pants on one side of their body and a dress on the other side. The only time I ever saw a person look like this was Halloween 1984, when my friend Billy showed up at a party as half man and half woman. He did the half beard thing and everything. It was very creative. However, giving people the impression that transgender individuals are "half men and half women" is not accurate and not cool.

Aliens

 Really? This stuff already confuses lots of people. Let's keep it human.

Whatever, Just Wash Your Hands

I actually think this sign is a laugh riot, and the first time I saw it I had to take a pic and send it to all of my friends. It's a humorous and snarky reaction to the current restroom hubbub, which I personally appreciate. However, the "All-Gender Restroom" sign is more professional, more timeless, and, in the end, probably best.

All-Gender Restroom

Sam Killermann, author of *A Guide to Gender* and creator of the website It's Pronounced Metrosexual (https://www.itspronouncedmetrosexual.com, a truly wonderful resource for all things gender), created a very simple all-gender restroom sign. You can print it free of charge at http://www.guidetogender.com/toilet/.

NOTES

1. Some of the information offered in this section comes from the Joint Commission, *Advancing Effective Communication, Cultural Competence, and Patient- and Family-Centered Care for the Lesbian, Gay, Bisexual, and Transgender (LGBT) Community: A Field Guide* (Oak Brook, IL: Joint Commission, 2011), https://www.joint commission.org/assets/1/18/LGBTFieldGuide.pdf.

2. Michael Sadowski, *Safe Is Not Enough: Better Schools for LGBTQ Students* (Cambridge, MA: Harvard Education Press, 2016), 11.

3. National LGBT Health Education Center, *Focus on Forms and Policy: Creating an Inclusive Environment for LGBT Patients*, https://www.lgbthealtheducation.org/wp-content/uploads/2017/08/Forms-and-Policy-Brief.pdf.

4. Human Rights Campaign, *Corporate Equality Index 2019*, last updated April 4, 2019, https://assets2.hrc.org/files/assets/resources/CEI-2019-FullReport.pdf?_ga=2.72494480.2003376306.1571331256-1109047636.1571331256.

5. CNBC, "'Bathroom Bill' to Cost North Carolina $3.76 Billion," March, 27, 2017, https://www.cnbc.com/2017/03/27/bathroom-bill-to-cost-north-carolina-376-billion.html.

6. Jason Hanna, Madison Park, and Elliott C. McLaughlin, "North Carolina Repeals 'Bathroom Bill,'" CNN Politics, March 30, 2017, https://www.cnn.com/2017/03/30/politics/north-carolina-hb2-agreement/index.html.

7. Jackson Bird, "How to Talk (and Listen) to Transgender People," TED, June 2017, https://www.ted.com/talks/jackson_bird_how_to_talk_and_listen_to_transgender_people?language=en#t-15186.

8. Noah Michelson, "More Americans Claim to Have Seen a Ghost Than Have Met a Trans Person," *HuffPost*, December, 21, 2015, https://www.huffpost.com/entry/more-americans-claim-to-have-seen-a-ghost-than-have-met-a-trans-person_n_5677fee5e4b014efe0d5ed62.

9. Mitch Kellaway, "Trans Folks Respond to 'Bathroom Bills' with #WeJustNeedToPee Selfies," *Advocate*, March 14, 2015, https://www.advocate.com/politics/transgender/2015/03/14/trans-folks-respond-bathroom-bills-wejustneedtopcc-selfies.

TAKING IT TO THE STREETS

In the end, we will remember not the words of our enemies, but
the silence of our friends.

—Martin Luther King Jr.

Much of what I have shared in this book involves ways we can be respectful
in our language, effectively educate others, and advocate for change within
our workplaces, schools, faith communities, and social circles. This chapter
focuses on moving outside of these smaller circles with community efforts that
create political change, offer financial support to organizations, and celebrate the
LGBTQ+ communities.

PRIDE

I am not typically a fan of loud, crowded festivals and parades, but Pride truly
energizes me. In a world where 46 percent of LGBTQ+ people hide who they are
at work,[1] being able to be out, loud, proud, covered head to toe in rainbows, and
surrounded by supportive people for a few days out of the year can be truly liberat-
ing. I love to be a part of it. If you live in or near a city that runs Pride, volunteering
for this event to help make it as safe and as special as possible for our LGBTQ+
friends is a kind gift that allies can offer. You are also welcome, of course, to simply
rainbow up, flaunt your pride, and enjoy the event. I have never experienced a
Pride festival or parade that wasn't ally friendly and welcoming.

TALKING WITH POLITICIANS

"Wait—what? I have to talk to politicians?" No, you don't have to, but according to the website 5 Calls, a great online resource for connecting with your local politicians with ease and impact, calling is the most effective way to communicate your thoughts and concerns. Check out the website at http://www.5calls .org/ for information on helpful pointers for making calls, including a two-minute YouTube video called "How to Call Your Representative with 5calls.org." On PFLAG's website, "Advocacy One-Pagers" is another excellent resource for advocacy and lobbying.[2]

Still scared? I feel your pain. This is not my forte. That's why I contacted my go-to guy and founder of Acronym Project Noah Wagoner for some words of advice. "People are fine going to restaurants because they *know* the expected script," he says. "Table for four, follow host, figure out what to drink, figure out appetizers, figure out meal, eat, ask for refills, ask for bill, pay, tip, leave. Politics is just like that, except we haven't gotten a chance to practice it before (or not nearly the thousands of times we've done the restaurant script)."

Noah suggests that you write out what you want to say before you call, for example: "Hi. My name is Jeannie Gainsburg and I'm a constituent from [fill in your town name and/or zip code]. I am calling because LGBTQ+ people deserve legal protections on a national level. I strongly encourage [fill in politician's name] to support the Equality Act of 2019. Thank you for your help and your time."

When you make your call, you will simply state why you are calling in a sentence or two, either to an aide or a machine. You will not be expected to debate anyone. It's as simple as ordering a pizza, only instead of a warm pie you'll get a warm glow of pride from a job well done. And if this was really out-of-your-comfort-zone scary, consider rewarding yourself with the pizza! Self-care, baby!

RALLIES, MARCHES, PROTESTS, AND LOBBYING

Being with like-minded and active people at peaceful rallies, marches, protests, and lobbying events can be powerful. I once participated in a rally to support transgender people of color following a violent incident in my city. We gathered on a busy city street corner, held signs, and walked to a different corner every time the light changed. It was beautiful in its simplicity and powerful in its message.

I have also attended large, loud events like national marches, which have an entirely different feel and are super energizing. If you have never attended a rally or march, try one out and see if it's your thing, but do your homework ahead of time and be prepared. Find out who is organizing the event and what the expectations are for participants. Amnesty International has a helpful document on protests and marches, including what to do, what to bring, what to wear, and your rights as a protester.[3]

Lobby or advocacy days are organized with the purpose of visiting the state capitol and bringing awareness to state politicians about LGBTQ+ concerns. They provide an opportunity for LGBTQ+ community members and allies to voice their opinions to politicians and share the personal impact that polices have on them and their families. Often there is a focus for the day, like transgender rights or safe schools. Many times organizing agencies offer workshops on how to lobby effectively and provide bus transportation to and from the event. This is a great way to meet other LGBTQ+ activists, to stay informed about political issues relating to LGBTQ+ lives, and to practice your "talking with politicians" skills.

FUNDRAISING

I have never met anyone who likes fundraising. Most people hate asking family members and friends for money and would rather have a root canal. If you are one of these folks, *please* don't move on to the next chapter until you have read about my metamorphosis from a miserable and reluctant fundraiser to the coordinator of our LGBTQ+ center's most successful fundraising event.

Many years ago, two friends of mine (both straight, cisgender allies) decided that they needed an excuse to bike and drink beer. They proposed a bike ride fundraiser that raised money for the nonprofit LGBTQ+ agency where I was employed. That first year all I did was pedal in this bike ride and reluctantly ask my friends and family to support me. The ride took place in September 2010. We had eighteen riders. We rode one hundred kilometers. We raised $4,000. I lost track of the number of beers we consumed.

The next year my two friends didn't want to coordinate the ride again, so I decided to try my hand at it. I ended up coordinating the ride for the next eight years. This little bike ride fundraiser became my passion, pride, and joy. It grew and grew until our biggest year, when we had seventy-five riders and brought in $63,000 for our center.

Toward the end of my tenure as the ride coordinator I had consistently become the top fundraiser, typically bringing in between 8 and 10 percent of the total donations for the ride. Inevitably, I became a fundraising coach for others who didn't want to "make the ask." Here are some things I learned along the way:

- People are inspired by heartfelt asks that talk about what the money will be used for and why you are involved.
- Fundraising far and wide connected me to tons of allies I never knew existed.
- Lots of folks were truly grateful to have an opportunity to make a difference and ended up thanking *me* for giving them the opportunity to support a great cause. Asking, giving, humanity, vulnerability, grace, and love are all intertwined. I learned this from singer, songwriter, and author Amanda Palmer. If you're not convinced, consider watching her TED Talk "The Art of Asking." Even better, read her book by the same title, which opens with the sentences, "Who's got a tampon? I just got my period."[4]
- Having a hook or a gimmick can put the "fun" back in fundraising. One of my more creative gimmicks was writing on my body, in permanent marker, the name of every person who donated to my fundraising page so they could come along with me on the ride. For a donation of $50 or more my donors got to pick their body part. Ooh-la-la!

Fundraisers are an excellent way for allies to connect with other allies and to offer support for LGBTQ+ organizations and school clubs. Don't shy away from fundraising. Have some fun! Deliver homemade cookies to the door of your top donor. Dye your hair blue if you make your fundraising goal. What are *you* willing to do for a donation?

NOTES

1. Human Rights Campaign, *A Workplace Divided: Understanding the Climate for LGBTQ Workers Nationwide*, https://www.hrc.org/resources/a-workplace-divided -understanding-the-climate-for-lgbtq-workers-nationwide.

2. 5calls.org, "How to Call Your Representative with 5calls.org," https://www.you tube.com/watch?v=N62ViRRn61I. PFLAG, "Advocacy One-Pagers," https://pflag.org/ resource/advocacy-one-pagers.

3. Amnesty International, "Safety during Protest" [flyer], https://www.amnestyusa .org/pdfs/SafeyDuringProtest_F.pdf.

4. Amanda Palmer, "The Art of Asking," speech given at TED2013 in February 2013, https://www.ted.com/talks/amanda_palmer_the_art_of_asking?language=en; *The Art of Asking: Or How I Learned to Stop Worrying and Let People Help* (New York: Grand Central, 2014).

Part IV

ALLYING RESPONSIBLY

ALLY BACKLASH

Allyship is not showing the world how good you are being, it is showing the world how backwards it is.

—Jay Dodd

If you are already out there doing good work as an ally, you are probably already aware that there is such a thing as backlash against allies. If you're new to the game, please don't get discouraged. There are good reasons why people within marginalized communities might be disenchanted with people who identify as allies. Bad allyship has caused bad feelings. In this chapter I'll discuss some of the most common areas of backlash against allies. With any luck, you will all pop out the other end feeling even more empowered to get involved and to do the job right!

ALLY IS A LABEL, NOT AN IDENTITY

In chapter 5 we talked about how we should not label people. We should listen to the words they use to identify themselves and then mirror those terms. Well, the word *ally* is an exception, kind of like the word *receipt*, which doesn't follow the "i before e, except after c" rule. When it comes to *ally*, it's helpful to think of it less as an identity and more as something someone says about you, if you're doing it right.

I was chatting recently with a friend over lunch. They were upset because someone at work, who has been blocking their efforts to create a more inclusive space, kept saying, "Look, you know I'm an ally." My friend said it was as if he was using his ally identity as a pass that allowed him to steamroll ahead with some pretty transphobic policies. In my friend's opinion, no one should ever identify as an ally. They should just do the work for change; if someone calls another person an ally, then that's a really nice compliment.

In the essay "No More 'Allies'" from her book *Black Girl Dangerous*, Mia McKenzie writes, "I will no longer use the term 'ally' to describe anyone. Instead, I'll use the phrase 'currently operating in solidarity with.' Or something. I mean, yeah, it's clunky as hell. But it gets at something that the label of 'ally' just doesn't. And that's this: actions count; labels don't."[1]

On a practical level, using "currently operating in solidarity with" is challenging. It would have been extremely difficult to write this book without using the word *ally*. Writing "currently operating in solidarity with the LGBTQ+ communities" doesn't fit very well on a pin. So the reality is that I do use the identity term *ally* to describe myself. You may decide to as well. But I think it's incredibly important for us to understand the pushback against the term. If we ever catch ourselves thinking, "It's okay for me to say that or do this because I'm an ally," we're doing it wrong.

Thinking of the word *ally* as a gift or a compliment that is given to us, rather than who we are, also helps us to remember that being an ally is about action. It's not a static identity that we wear on a badge: "Ta-da! I did it! Pop the champagne! I'm an ally!" It's about doing stuff and constantly learning.

In her essay "Fluid and Imperfect Ally Positioning: Some Gifts of Queer Theory," Vikki Reynolds writes, "I am always becoming an ally. I am continually being woken up to my locations of privilege."[2]

Here's the good news: Every time someone is pleased with the work you are doing toward inclusion and calls you an ally, I give you my full blessing to pat yourself on the back and pop one of those mini champagnes or a soda to celebrate!

SHUT UP AND LISTEN

I have been to many social justice events, workshops, and rallies where allies were told to "shut up and listen." If and when you hear this, I hope you will do these four things:

1. Be kind to yourself. In your head, remove the "shut up" from this statement and focus on the "listen."

2. Assume good intent. Think about where this anger, frustration, and snarkiness are coming from. If a community of people feels the need to tell allies to "shut up and listen," it means that they have repeatedly been in situations where professed allies have used their voices to talk over people within the community. If we are involved in social justice work because we want to create change, then we need to make sure that we are letting the people within the marginalized communities lead the way and that they are the ones deciding what that change should look like.

3. Remember, it's not your story. Remind yourself that as allies, we will *never* understand what it's like to be a part of the marginalized group we are advocating for. We can and should read about, watch videos on, and listen to the experiences of people in those groups, but we will never have that lived experience.

4. Make your choices. *You* get to decide which groups you will advocate for and support. If you feel that you are being treated in a disrespectful way and because of this you cannot get on board with a specific group or movement, peace out. Find groups to work with whose mission statements and messaging feel right for you.

"A" IS FOR ASEXUAL

Sometimes we see the initialism written as: LGBTQA, LGBTQA+, or LGBTQIA. When there is only one "A," does it stand for *asexual* or *ally*? The answer is that it depends on who wrote it. Some people feel that the "A" always stands for *asexual* and that *ally* should never be included in the initialism.

Honestly, when I first heard someone say that *ally* should not be included in the initialism, I got my trousers in a twist and thought it was pretty darn anti-ally. But then I did some research and looked into what was going on, and actually it makes sense. Sydney Lynn wrote in the article "The A Stands for Asexuality: Putting the A in the LGBTQA+ Community" that allies aren't "part of the community"; they are "part of the movement."[3] Can't argue with that: The definition of an ally is someone who is *not* a part of a particular marginalized group but who stands up for and advocates for the rights of people in that group.

Another point to think about is that it must surely cause some discontent to have "A" for *ally* represented in the initialism, when many people within the LGBTQ+ communities still aren't represented. If LGBTQA+ stands for lesbian, gay, bisexual, transgender, queer, ally, plus so much more, and I'm intersex (part of that "so much more"), I might be a bit annoyed that *ally* got a letter and I didn't.

One final thought on this topic is that most people who are a part of a marginalized group know that sometimes getting together in your [fill in the blank]-only space is empowering, rejuvenating, and typically less exhausting than being in spaces where not everyone "gets it." If the "A" stands for *ally*, then how do we distinguish between the spaces where allies are welcome and the ones where we aren't? If there is only one "A" in the initialism, it's probably best to assume that it stands for *asexual*. If you're not sure if an event is open to allies, connect with the event coordinator and ask.

KEY ALLY TAKEAWAYS

I hope, having read about the most common pushback points against allies, you are feeling empowered to be the best ally that you can be. In summary, here are some basic principles of good allyship:

- Think of the word *ally* as a compliment, something you earn with your actions, not an identity that gives you privileges.
- Be mindful of the fact that you are part of the movement, not part of the community.
- Respect spaces and events where marginalized people gather and allies are asked not to attend.
- When invited into LGBTQ+ spaces, listen to the people in the communities and let them guide your support efforts.
- Support and advocate for groups and movements that feel right and are a good fit for you.
- Be kind to yourself. (See chapter 13 for some suggestions if you stink at this.)

PAY IT FORWARD

When I began my work as a straight cisgender ally to the LGBTQ+ communities I was very fearful of pushback against me. Although there have been a few minor "anti-ally" incidents here and there, there have been many, many more situations where I have been welcomed with open arms into the LGBTQ+ rights movement. Early on my heart was in the right place, but I was ignorant of the correct terms and unaware of the issues. I needed a lot of hand-holding, and thankfully, I got it. If LGBTQ+ community members had not thanked me for the efforts I was making, had not answered my silly questions, and had not offered me words of encouragement, I would not have become the education director at our local LGBTQ+ center and I would not have written this book.

What I like to do now, whenever I can, is pay that gift of kindness and patience forward. When I am in a position as the educator, either as a more experienced ally to a newbie or as a woman to a man who is learning how to be an ally to the women's rights movement, I can tell people to "shut up and listen," or I can take the opportunity to thank them for their efforts, kindly answer their questions, and offer a hand of support. I choose the latter. I hope you will too.

NOTES

1. Mia McKenzie, *Black Girl Dangerous: On Race, Queerness, Class and Gender* (Oakland, CA: BGD Press, 2014).

2. Vikki Reynolds, "Fluid and Imperfect Ally Positioning: Some Gifts of Queer Theory," *Context*, October 15, 2010, https://www.suu.edu/allies/pdf/reynolds.pdf.

3. Sydney Lynn, "The A Stands for Asexuality: Putting the A in the LGBTQA+ Community," *Thought Catalog*, April 3, 2015, https://thoughtcatalog.com/sydney-lynn/2015/04/the-a-stands-for-asexuality-putting-the-a-in-lgbtqa-community/.

SUSTAINABILITY

*Caring for myself is not self-indulgence, it is self-preservation,
and that is an act of political warfare.*

Audre Lorde

Being an LGBTQ+ person is not a choice, but being an ally is. One of the reasons I was motivated to write this book was to offer a practical, encouraging, and useful guide for being an ally to the LGBTQ+ communities. Workshops and books for allies often tell you what you *must* do, feature a daunting list of expectations, and imply that if you do not hold yourself accountable to every single one, you are not a true ally. I find these workshops and books intimidating and unrealistic. Instead of motivating allies to be better and more involved, I believe they have the opposite effect, convincing people that they are never going to be "ally enough" and discouraging them from even trying.

I was fortunate to be able to turn being an ally into a full-time career, but the reality is that most people can't. Typically there are jobs, children, homes, and pets that need our attention during the majority of our waking hours. With an unyielding list of expectations and an unforgiving attitude when people mess up, who would ever willingly choose to be an ally with all of these other things vying for our time? If we are going to add allyship to the long list of other life obligations and choices, then we must do it wisely, so that it fits into our lives in a way that is sustainable. This chapter offers some pointers for how to do that.

TAKE CARE OF YOURSELF

Caring for yourself is critical to your work as an effective ally. Below are some suggestions for how to care for yourself when ally life gets challenging.

Be on Your Own Team

Be aware of your needs and take them seriously. Here is an example of how I take care of myself after I facilitate a full-day workshop. At the end of these sessions, I am exhausted and vulnerable. I have been on my feet for over ten hours, I have taken care of my participants' emotional and physical needs, I have worked to keep the energy in the room up, and I have put my heart and soul into the workshop. I know that a helpful tip from a workshop evaluation on how I can improve, which, the next morning over coffee, will have me nodding my head and thinking, "That's a great suggestion," could have me in tears the night of the workshop. So I take that pile of evaluations and set it aside for the morning. Then I take care of me for the rest of the night. Are there self-care gifts you can give yourself when you're exhausted and vulnerable?

Treat Yourself the Way You Would Treat Your Best Friend

If you have a tendency to be hard on yourself when you mess up, think about what you would say to your best friend if they were in the same situation. Then say that to yourself.

Give Yourself Permission to Fail

Recently, I have gotten into indoor rock climbing. Completing a climb without falling feels amazing! However, I know that if I never fall, my rate of improvement will be slower than if I push myself to try more challenging climbs and fail. Failure and mistakes are essential to learning and growth. Keep this in mind and give yourself permission to be human, mess up, and learn from your mistakes.

Use Positive Self-Coaching Tips

Unfortunately, negative self-talk ("Ugh! I'm such a loser!") often comes very naturally to people, but positive self-talk ("It's okay; I'm human") doesn't. Think about some positive self-coaching tips that can help you through tough times. Have you done something super adventurous or gutsy? Remind yourself of that the next time you're in a situation where you're intimidated. I like to think back to when I went skydiving with my daughter and use this motivator: "Jeannie, you jumped out of a frickin' airplane! Don't let *this* scare you." Is there something a loved one says to you that calms you when you're stressed? Try saying that to yourself when you're in a difficult situation. I am claustrophobic. I recently got through an hour-long MRI by imagining my husband, Ed, next to me on one side, saying, "You're okay, baby" and my best friend, Pam, on the other side, saying, "You've got this."

Know Your Recipe for Happiness and Follow It

When I travel for work and my usual routine gets thrown out of whack for several days, my recipe for happiness and self-care involves three things: sleep, exercise, and vegetables. If I consistently only get one of these during my travels, I'm in pretty rough shape. Two is significantly better. All three and I am at the top of my game! What's your happiness recipe?

Think about What's Not Wrong

Have you ever noticed that comfort is such a fantastic feeling immediately after a toothache? But do we appreciate comfort on a daily basis? In his book *Peace Is Every Step*, world-renowned Zen master and spiritual leader Thích Nhất Hạnh talks about the importance of spending some time thinking about what's not wrong in any given moment. He writes, "We often ask, 'What's wrong?' Doing so, we invite painful seeds of sorrow to come up and manifest. We feel suffering, anger, and depression, and produce more such seeds. We would be much happier if we tried to stay in touch with the healthy, joyful seeds inside us and around us. We should learn to ask, 'What's not wrong?' and be in touch with that."[1]

When life gets challenging, I remind myself to focus on what's not wrong. For example:

What's wrong: My car broke down and I'm late for a meeting. Darn it!
What's not wrong: I'm healthy! My family is healthy! Paying for car repairs won't be a huge financial burden for me! The sun is out! I've got a granola bar in my bag! I hate meetings! I don't have to poop! Life is good!

Even during very challenging times you are likely to find that there is so much more that is not wrong with your life.

PACE YOURSELF

Part of being an effective ally and really sticking with it for the long haul involves figuring out what works for you, what interests you, what you will and won't do, and what reasonably fits into your schedule and lifestyle. Ed and I are pretty good about exercising almost every day, but we have very different strategies for making that work for us. Ed is motivated by his gear and his data. He uses his Garmin watch, his "smart trainer," and the Zwift and Strava apps. He calculates his heart rate, his calories burned, his miles per hour, his pedal revolutions per minute, and I don't know what else. I listen to my music and plod down the street or I watch a movie while I pedal on my exercise bike. I couldn't care less how fast I am going, how many calories I'm burning, or whether or not I am performing better than I did yesterday. If I had to calculate my CPMs, my MPHs, and my RPMs, I simply wouldn't exercise. I'd lie on the couch instead, watching *Star Trek: The Next Generation* reruns.

I have come to learn my strengths and interests as an ally as well. I love having respectful conversations with people. I love creating spaces for individuals to be vulnerable with each other without fear of judgment. I hate talking to politicians. I *really* hate it. Through all of my years volunteering and working at our LGBTQ+ center, I went only once to an LGBTQ+ lobbying day at our state capitol. Does dropping that piece off my plate make me a bad ally? I don't think so. I think the other work I do makes up for the fact that I skip out on a day that will make me completely miserable.

I am not advocating for never moving out of our comfort zones. I am all about trying new things and challenging ourselves. My point is that we can't do everything, and we should not be expected to. It's not realistic or sustainable to have those expectations. Extreme lose-weight-fast diets don't work. Small healthy eating lifestyle changes do. Give yourself permission to do what you love, what fits your personality, and what you are likely to be able to continue to do for the long haul.

CONTINUE YOUR EDUCATION

One very important aspect of being a useful and effective ally is ensuring that we stay current on LGBTQ+ language and topics. This doesn't mean we need to know every single vocabulary word and identity, but we should work to keep up to date on what is happening within the communities we are advocating for. One way that I do this without becoming overwhelmed is to take words or topics one at a time. If I hear about an issue or an identity that's unfamiliar to me more than once or twice, I investigate it and educate myself. For example, I knew the dictionary definition of the word *asexual*, but I really didn't know much about this identity or community. About eight years ago, I noticed that workshop participants were suddenly asking questions about asexual people. It was time for me to educate myself. I did some reading, I watched some videos, and I also watched the documentary film (*A*)*sexual*.[2] I learned a lot, and it really helped me understand the differences between sexual attraction and romantic attraction. I became much more proficient at answering questions about the asexual community in a respectful and informed way.

Besides consuming books, blogs, videos, and movies, we can also increase our ally savviness by getting out to events like workshops and conferences. The largest and best-known LGBTQ+ conference in the United States is Creating Change, an annual conference run by the National LGBTQ Task Force. It takes place in late January or early February in a different city each year. Not only does Creating Change offer a wide range of valuable workshops, but the venue itself turns into "queer planet" for five days. Hotel staff members walk around wearing pronoun pins, people introduce themselves by saying, "Hi! I'm Jeannie—she, her, and hers," and entire floors of restrooms are designated all-gender. It's an extremely cool experience and exposes participants to the most cutting-edge stuff.

EVERY SO OFTEN, RETURN TO "WHY?"

I mentioned in chapter 11 that for eight years I was the coordinator of our agency's bike ride fundraiser. One year, while trying to encourage the riders to get out there and start fundraising, I implemented a "Why I Ride" campaign. I asked riders to snap a picture of themselves holding a sign about why they ride and post it on their social media sites and in their fundraising e-mails. The results were passionate, moving, and effective.

Six days before that year's ride in June 2016, the Pulse nightclub shooting in Orlando took place. Fifty-three people were wounded and forty-nine were killed. It stands as the deadliest attack ever on the LGBTQ+ communities.

Every year I give a brief speech before the riders set off to motivate them for the day ahead. That year, with an extremely heavy heart, I found it more difficult than ever to inspire my crew. I had no words. I agonized for days over what I would say, and in the end it was my riders and their "Why I Ride" messages that inspired *me*. Instead of a speech that year, I read their beautiful messages.

Here are a few of the reasons my riders took to the road in June 2016:

Joe: I ride because I don't want my nephew to grow up in a world where people are discriminated against for whom they love and how they identify.

Debbie: I ride for health, because hiding who you are is not healthy.

Pam: I ride for truth. I can't imagine how it must feel to be afraid to let your true self show. And until that fear becomes groundless, I will ride.

Craig: I ride because equality means everyone!

Anastasia: I ride because this is the only world we have and I want it to be a safezone for everyone. #loveeveryone #somechicksmarrychicks #getoverit #fckh8

Ronald: I ride because LGBT youth and elderly still experience huge injustices.

Rowan: I ride for everyone who never will again. Remember our dead and fight like hell for the living.

Maya: I ride because love and equity are the foundation for happiness.

I told you at the very beginning that this is a book about how to be an ally, not why to be an ally—but pause every once in a while and think about why you do the work you do. Talk with other allies about what motivates them. It is powerful, restorative, and necessary.

Jeannie: I ride because if my grandchildren ever ask me if I was involved in the fight for LGBTQ+ rights, I'll get to say, "Hell yeah!"

Enjoy the ride.

NOTES

1. Thích Nhất Hạnh, *Peace Is Every Step: The Path of Mindfulness in Everyday Life* (New York: Bantam Books, 1991), 77.

2. Katy Chevigny, Beth Davenport, and Jolene Pinder (producers) and Angela Tucker (director), *(A)sexual* (New York: FilmBuff, 2012), DVD.

GLOSSARY

Cultural words and identity words vary in meaning depending on the user. They also change over time. This glossary should be used as a tool for basic reference. It should never be used to label others. Proceed with caution!

affectional orientation: The part of an individual's identity that describes to whom they are romantically attracted. It is also known as *romantic orientation*.

agender: Relating to an individual who has no gender.

ally: A person who is not a part of a particular marginalized group but who stands up for and advocates for the rights of people in that group.

androgynous: A gender expression that is neither feminine nor masculine. It is sometimes defined as a blending of both masculinity and femininity.

aromantic: Relating to an individual with a low or absent romantic attraction.

asexual: Relating to an individual with a low or absent sexual attraction.

binary: Relating to two things or two options. Individuals who identify their gender as either *man* or *woman* fit into the gender binary.

biological sex: Relating to an individual's reproductive system and secondary sex characteristics: genitalia, chromosomes, hormones, etc.

biphobia: Fear, intolerance, or hatred of people who are, or who are perceived to be, bisexual or pansexual.

biromantic: Relating to an individual who is romantically attracted to both men and women, or to more than one gender.

bisexual: Relating to an individual who is sexually attracted to both men and women, or to more than one gender.

cisgender: Relating to an individual whose gender identity matches the sex they were assigned at birth; someone who is not transgender.

cisnormativity: The assumption that everyone is cisgender or that being cisgender is the "right" way to be.

cross-dresser: An individual who, for comfort, enjoyment, and/or self-expression, wears clothing that has been designated by society as inappropriate for their gender.

drag king: An entertainer whose act features wearing men's clothing, facial makeup, and facial hair in order to impersonate a man.

drag queen: An entertainer whose act features wearing women's clothing, a wig, and makeup in order to impersonate a woman.

gay: Relating to an individual who is sexually attracted only to people of the same gender. Traditionally a term used only by men, it is now embraced by some women as well.

gender expansive: Relating to an individual whose gender expression and/or gender identity does not fit into society's binary expectations. Some people prefer this term to *gender nonconforming*.

gender expression: The way an individual expresses their gender to the outside world, through clothing, hairstyles, interests, mannerisms, and movement. It is typically labeled as *masculine, feminine,* or *androgynous*.

gender-fluid: Relating to an individual whose gender identity regularly fluctuates.

gender identity: An individual's sense of their own gender, typically identified as *man, woman,* or *nonbinary*.

gender nonconforming: Relating to an individual whose gender expression and/or gender identity does not fit into society's binary expectations. Some people prefer this term to *gender expansive*.

gender policing: The societal enforcement of binary gender roles and expectations.

genderqueer: Relating to an individual whose gender identity is neither man nor woman.

hermaphrodite: An outdated and derogatory term for a person born with atypical genitalia. The word *intersex*, which is broader in its definition, is a more respectful term.

heteronormativity: The assumption that everyone is heterosexual or that being heterosexual is the "right" way to be.

heteroromantic: Relating to a man who is romantically attracted only to women, or a woman who is romantically attracted only to men.

heterosexual: Relating to a man who is sexually attracted only to women, or a woman who is sexually attracted only to men; also known as *straight*.

homophobia: Fear, intolerance, or hatred of people who are, or who are perceived to be, gay or lesbian.

homoromantic: Relating to an individual who is romantically attracted only to people of the same gender.

homosexual: A dated term relating to an individual who is sexually attracted only to people of the same gender. The words *gay* and *lesbian* are more respectful terms.

intersectionality: The complex and overlapping ways that an individual's many identities (sexual orientation, gender, race, ethnicity, ability, socioeconomic status, immigration status, language, size, religion, etc.) come together and shape their experiences and interactions. Prejudice and discrimination related to these overlapping identities are unique and are different from prejudice and discrimination faced by people with each individual identity.

intersex: Relating to an individual whose chromosomes and/or biological sex characteristics (i.e., genitals, reproductive organs, and/or hormones, etc.) are not typical.

intimate behaviors: Sexual and/or romantic activities.

lesbian: Relating to a woman who is sexually attracted only to women.

LGBTQ+: One of the many initialisms created to express all sexual and gender minorities. It stands for lesbian, gay, bisexual, transgender, queer and/or questioning, plus so much more!

microaggression: A commonplace comment or behavior toward a marginalized group that is hurtful, insulting, or demeaning. The comment may or may not be intentionally insulting.

misgender: To use an incorrect gendered term when referring to someone.

MSM: An abbreviation for "men who have sex with men." This term was created to acknowledge and offer appropriate healthcare to men who do not identify as *gay, bisexual,* or *pansexual* but who are engaging in sexual activities with men.

nonbinary: Relating to an individual whose gender identity is neither man nor woman. This can also be used as an umbrella term that includes many identities, such as agender, gender expansive, gender-fluid, genderqueer, and Two-Spirit.

panromantic: Relating to an individual who is romantically attracted to people regardless of their gender.

pansexual: Relating to an individual who is sexually attracted to people regardless of their gender.

polyamorous: Relating to an individual who engages in more than one sexual and/or romantic relationship at a time, with the knowledge and consent of all involved.

queer: A reclaimed term that is liked by some and disliked by others. It can be used to define any orientation that is not straight or any gender that is not cisgender.

questioning: Relating to an individual who is currently unsure of or exploring their orientation and/or gender identity.

romantic orientation: The part of an individual's identity that describes to whom they are romantically attracted. It is also known as *affectional orientation*.

same-gender loving: An identity term used within some communities of color relating to individuals who are attracted to people of the same gender.

sexual orientation: The part of an individual's identity that describes to whom they are sexually attracted.

straight: Relating to a man who is sexually attracted only to women, or a woman who is sexually attracted only to men; also known as *heterosexual*.

transgender: Relating to an individual whose sex assigned at birth does not match their gender identity. This word can also be used as an umbrella term that includes many identities, such as genderqueer, nonbinary, trans man, and trans woman.

transition: Changing from one state to another. Often used to refer to the process by which a transgender individual takes steps to align their body and their gender identity.

trans man: Relating to an individual who was assigned female at birth, but whose gender identity is male.

transphobia: Fear, intolerance, or hatred of people who are, or who are perceived to be, transgender.

transsexual: A dated term relating to an individual who uses medical and/or surgical treatments to help align their body with their gender identity by transitioning from the sex they were assigned at birth. The newer words *transgender* and *trans* are more commonly used, whether or not a person undergoes a medical or surgical transition.

transvestite: A dated term for an individual who enjoys wearing clothing that has been designated by society as inappropriate for their gender. The word *cross-dresser* is a more respectful term.

trans woman: Relating to an individual who was assigned male at birth, but whose gender identity is female.

Two-Spirit: A modern term, created in 1990, that may be used by Indigenous North Americans as an LGBTQ+ identity term or to describe people who have the spirit of both man and woman and/or are a third gender. It is embraced by some Indigenous North Americans and rejected by others. The term may be defined differently depending on the community or tribe.

BIBLIOGRAPHY

AAA Project Visibility. *Project Visibility*. Boulder, CO: Boulder County Area Agency on Aging, 2004. DVD.

Amnesty International. "Safety during Protest" [flyer]. https://www.amnestyusa.org/pdfs/SafeyDuringProtest_F.pdf.

Arana, Gabriel. "The Truth about Gay Men and Pedophilia." *INTO*, November 16, 2017. https://www.intomore.com/impact/The-Truth-About-Gay-Men-and-Pedophilia.

Ayvazian, Andrea. "Creating Conversations: Becoming a White Ally." Filmed at Greenfield Community College, Greenfield, MA, November 23, 2010. https://www.youtube.com/watch?v=yXZPHc6MkLI.

Beckham, Ash. "I am SO GAY." Speech given at Ignite Boulder, Boulder, CO, March 2, 2013. http://www.ignitetalks.io/videos/i-am-so-gay.

Bird, Jackson. "How to Talk (and Listen) to Transgender People." TED, June 2017. https://www.ted.com/talks/jackson_bird_how_to_talk_and_listen_to_transgender_people?language=en#t-15186.

Bornstein, Kate. *Gender Outlaw*. New York: Vintage Books, 1995.

Cass, Vivienne. "Homosexual Identity Formation: A Theoretical Model." *Journal of Homosexuality* 4, no. 3 (spring 1979): 219–35. https://www.ncbi.nlm.nih.gov/pubmed/264126.

Chevigny, Katy, Beth Davenport, and Jolene Pinder (producers) and Angela Tucker (director). *(A)sexual*. New York: FilmBuff, 2012. DVD.

Clarey, Christopher. "Gender Test after a Gold-Medal Finish." *New York Times*, August 19, 2009. https://www.nytimes.com/2009/08/20/sports/20runner.html.

Clark, Dorie. "North Carolina's Bathroom Bill Repeal Won't Bring the NCAA Back." *Fortune*, March 30, 2017. http://fortune.com/2017/03/30/north-carolina-bathroom -bill-hb2-hb142-repeal-ncaa-lgbt/.

CNBC. "'Bathroom Bill' to Cost North Carolina $3.76 Billion." March, 27, 2017. https://www.cnbc.com/2017/03/27/bathroom-bill-to-cost-north-carolina-376-billion .html.

Colapinto, John. *As Nature Made Him: The Boy Who Was Raised as a Girl.* New York: HarperCollins, 2000.

Crenshaw, Kimberlé. "The Urgency of Intersectionality." Speech given at TEDWomen 2016, December 7, 2016. https://www.ted.com/talks/kimberle_crenshaw_the_ur gency_of_intersectionality?language=en.

Fearing, Scott. *Successful GLBT Education: A Manual.* Minneapolis: OutFront Minnesota, 1996.

Fox, Catherine O., and Tracy E. Ore. "(Un) Covering Normalized Gender and Race Subjectivities in LGBT 'Safe Spaces'." *Feminist Studies* 36, no. 3 (fall 2010): 629–49.

Hanna, Jason, Madison Park, and Eliott C. McLaughlin. "North Carolina Repeals 'Bathroom Bill'." CNN Politics, March 30, 2017. https://www.cnn.com/2017/03/30/ politics/north-carolina-hb2-agreement/index.html.

Hasenbush, Amira. "What Does Research Suggest about Transgender Restroom Policies?" *Education Week*, June 8, 2016. https://www.edweek.org/ew/articles/2016/ 06/08/what-does-research-suggest-about-transgender-restroom.html.

Herek, Gregory M. "Facts about Homosexuality and Child Molestation." Sexual Orientation: Science, Education, and Policy. https://psychology.ucdavis.edu/rainbow/html/ facts_molestation.html.

Hida. "How Common Is Intersex? An Explanation of the Stats." Intersex Campaign for Equality, April 1, 2015. https://www.intersexequality.com/how-common-is-intersex -in-humans/.

Human Rights Campaign (HRC). *Corporate Equality Index 2019.* Last updated April 4, 2019. https://assets2.hrc.org/files/assets/resources/CEI-2019-FullReport.pdf?_ ga=2.72494480.2003376306.1571331256-1109047636.1571331256.

———. "The Lies and Dangers of Efforts to Change Sexual Orientation or Gender Identity." https://www.hrc.org/resources/the-lies-and-dangers-of-reparative-therapy.

———. "State Maps of Laws & Policies." https://www.hrc.org/state-maps/.

———. "Violence against the Transgender Community in 2018." https://www.hrc.org/ resources/violence-against-the-transgender-community-in-2018.

———. "A Workplace Divided: Understanding the Climate for LGBTQ Workers Nationwide." https://assets2.hrc.org/files/assets/resources/AWorkplaceDivided-2018 .pdf?_ga=2.74196113.2003376306.1571331256-1109047636.1571331256.

———. "Workplace Gender Transition Guidelines." https://www.hrc.org/resources/ workplace-gender-transition-guidelines.

James, S. E., J. L. Herman, S. Rankin, et al. *The Report of the 2015 U.S. Transgender Survey*. Washington, DC: National Center for Transgender Equality, 2016. https://transequality.org/sites/default/files/docs/usts/USTS-Full-Report-Dec17.pdf.

The Joint Commission. *Advancing Effective Communication, Cultural Competence, and Patient- and Family-Centered Care for the Lesbian, Gay, Bisexual, and Transgender (LGBT) Community: A Field Guide*. Oak Brook, IL: Joint Commission, 2011. https://www.jointcommission.org/assets/1/18/LGBTFieldGuide.pdf.

Kann, Laura, Emily O'Malley Olsen, Tim McManus, et al. "Sexual Identity, Sex of Sexual Contacts, and Health-Related Behaviors among Students in Grades 9–12—United States and Selected Sites, 2015." *Center for Disease Control and Prevention Morbidity and Mortality Weekly Report, Surveillance Summaries* 65, no. 9 (August 12, 2016): 1–208. https://www.cdc.gov/mmwr/volumes/65/ss/pdfs/ss6509.pdf.

Keir, John (producer), and Grant Lahood (director). *Intersexion: Gender Ambiguity Unveiled*. Kilbirnie, Wellington, New Zealand: Ponsonby Production Limited, 2012. DVD

Kellaway, Mitch. "Trans Folks Respond to 'Bathroom Bills' with #WeJustNeedToPee Selfies." *Advocate*, March 14, 2015. https://www.advocate.com/politics/transgender/2015/03/14/trans-folks-respond-bathroom-bills-wejustneedtopee-selfies.

Keneally, Thomas. *Schindler's List*. New York: Simon & Schuster, 1982.

Khazan, Olga. "Milo Yiannopoulos and the Myth of the Gay Pedophile." *Atlantic*, February 21, 2017. https://www.theatlantic.com/health/archive/2017/02/milo-yiannopoulos-and-the-myth-of-the-gay-pedophile/517332/.

Killermann, Sam. *A Guide to Gender: The Social Justice Advocate's Handbook*. Revised and updated edition. Austin, TX: Impetus Books, 2017.

———. "Printable All-Gender Restroom Sign." A Guide to Gender. http://www.guidetogender.com/toilet/.

Kreps, Daniel. "Bruce Springsteen Cancels North Carolina Gig to Protest 'Bathroom Bill'." *Rolling Stone*, April 8, 2016. https://www.rollingstone.com/music/music-news/bruce-springsteen-cancels-north-carolina-gig-to-protest-bathroom-bill-227635/.

Lynn, Sydney. "The A Stands for Asexuality: Putting the A in the LGBTQA+ Community." *Thought Catalog*, April 3, 2015. https://thoughtcatalog.com/sydney-lynn/2015/04/the-a-stands-for-asexuality-putting-the-a-in-lgbtqa-community/.

Manji, Irshad. *Don't Label Me: An Incredible Conversation for Divided Times*. New York: St. Martin's Press, 2019.

McKenzie, Mia. *Black Girl Dangerous: On Race, Queerness, Class and Gender*. Oakland, CA: BGD Press, 2014.

Michelson, Noah. "More Americans Claim to Have Seen a Ghost Than Have Met a Trans Person." *HuffPost*, December 21, 2015. https://www.huffpost.com/entry/more-americans-claim-to-have-seen-a-ghost-than-have-met-a-trans-person_n_5677fee5e4b014efe0d5ed62.

Moreau, Julie. "No Link between Trans-Inclusive Policies and Bathroom Safety, Study Finds." NBC News, September 19, 2018. https://www.nbcnews.com/feature/nbc -out/no-link-between-trans-inclusive-policies-bathroom-safety-study-finds-n911106.

Myers, Alex. "Why We Need More Queer Identity Labels, Not Fewer." *Slate*, January 16, 2018. https://slate.com/human-interest/2018/01/lgbtq-people-need-more-labels -not-fewer.html.

National LGBT Health Education Center. *Focus on Forms and Policy: Creating an Inclusive Environment for LGBT Patients*. https://www.lgbthealtheducation.org/wp -content/uploads/2017/08/Forms-and-Policy-Brief.pdf.

Nhất Hạnh, Thích. *Peace Is Every Step: The Path of Mindfulness in Everyday Life*. New York: Bantam Books, 1991.

"*Orange Is the New Black*'s Wonder Woman Laverne Cox on Being a Transgender Trailblazer." *RadioTimes*, July 26, 2015. https://www.radiotimes.com/news/2015-07 -26/orange-is-the-new-blacks-wonder-woman-laverne-cox-on-being-a-transgender -trailblazer/.

Out Alliance. "Being Respectful to LGBTQ+ People." Training handout.

———. "Is My Child LGBTQ+?" Training handout.

———. "Tips for Respectful Communication in the Face of Resistance." Training handout.

Owens-Reid, Dannielle, and Russo, Kristin. *This Is a Book for Parents of Gay Kids*. San Francisco: Chronicle Books, 2014.

Palmer, Amanda. "The Art of Asking." Speech given at TED2013 in February 2013. https://www.ted.com/talks/amanda_palmer_the_art_of_asking?language=en.

———. *The Art of Asking: Or How I Learned to Stop Worrying and Let People Help*. New York: Grand Central, 2014.

Patterson, Don. "40 Keys to Volleyball Greatness." *VolleyballUSA* (summer 2014): 38–41.

PFLAG. "Advocacy One-Pagers." https://pflag.org/resource/advocacy-one-pagers.

Reynolds, Vikki. "Fluid and Imperfect Ally Positioning: Some Gifts of Queer Theory." *Context*, October 2010, 13–17. https://www.suu.edu/allies/pdf/reynolds.pdf.

Sadowski, Michael. *Safe Is Not Enough: Better Schools for LGBTQ Students*. Cambridge, MA: Harvard Education Press, 2016.

Shively, Michael G., and John P. DeCecco. "Components of Sexual Identity." *Journal of Homosexuality* 3, no. 1 (1977): 41–48. https://www.tandfonline.com/doi/ abs/10.1300/J082v03n01_04.

Tackenberg, Rich (director). *Coming Out Party*. Studio City, CA: Ariztical Entertainment, 2003. DVD.

Tatum, Beverly Daniel. *Why Are All the Black Kids Sitting Together in the Cafeteria?* Revised and updated edition. New York: Basic Books, 2017.

Utt, Jamie. "So You Call Yourself an Ally: 10 Things All 'Allies' Need to Know." *Everyday Feminism*, November 8, 2013. https://everydayfeminism.com/2013/11/things-allies -need-to-know/.

Ward, Geoffrey C., and Ken Burns. *Not for Ourselves Alone*. New York: Alfred A. Knopf, 1999.

Wikipedia. "LGBT Rights by Country or Territory." Last edited June 2, 2019. https://en.wikipedia.org/wiki/LGBT_rights_by_country_or_territory.

———. "Microaggression." Last edited May 28, 2019. https://en.wikipedia.org/wiki/Microaggression.

ACKNOWLEDGMENTS

This book would not have been possible without the support, knowledge, time, and generosity of the people below. An *enormous* thank-you goes out to:

Ed Freedman, for encouraging all adventures and for giving the gift that started it all.

Julie Gainsburg, for the many hours you put into editing this book, for all the Oxford commas, and for being there for me no matter what.

Hayden Freedman, for listening to *every* voice and for showing me what truly inclusive diversity conversations look like.

Becca Gainsburg, for reminding me to reach higher and for making me laugh.

Vicki and Roy Gainsburg, for raising me in a household where equality was a no-brainer.

Pam Polashenski, for showing me what badassery truly looks like.

Scott Fearing, for sharing the "assume goodwill" philosophy that is at the heart of this book and for creating a safe space for me to come out as a loud and proud ally.

Noah Wagoner, for being my social justice go-to guy and for being an ally to the world.

The wonderful team at Rowman & Littlefield: Mark Kerr, Courtney Packard, Jessica McCleary, Karin Cholak, and Meghann French.

ACKNOWLEDGMENTS

My personal reviewers, editors, and advisors: Tim Ackroyd, Steve Brosnihan, Julie Buchanan, Oona Foxe, Tovia Freedman, Alice Glinert, Shimona Gorelick, Christopher Hennelly, Chris Hinesley, Elizabeth Olson, Anastasia Polashenski, Tallis Polashenski, Walter Polashenski, Bev Mondillo Wright, and Steve Wright.

Everyone who made this book come alive with their personal stories, insights, and experiences: Jason Ballard, Sam Cappiello, Rowan Collins, Maur DeLaney, Joe Doty, Daniel Fox, Todd Gordon, Gabrielle Hermosa, Sean Johnston, Mike Kelly, Matt Krueger, Eridan Maeder, Wanda Martinez-Johncox, Lore McSpadden, Kayden Eli Miller, Dee Murray, Manuel Peña, Maya Polashenski, Ronald Pratt, Craig Ronald, Gloria Ronga, Susan Rubin, Matt Tappon, Deborah Trubatch, Jonathan Wetherbee, Owen Zacharias, and Sara Zacharias.

And Carlos the cat, for all of the snuggle breaks and for letting me mess with your pronouns.

INDEX

ABOUT THE AUTHOR

Jeannie Gainsburg is an educational trainer and consultant in the field of LGBTQ+ inclusion and effective allyship. Formerly the education director at the Out Alliance in Rochester, New York, she has personally facilitated or cofacilitated more than five hundred trainings and workshops in more than twenty different states at corporations, colleges, government agencies, K–12 schools, hospitals, faith communities, and more. Gainsburg has a BA in psychology from Brown University and an MA in social work and social research from Bryn Mawr College. She was under the impression that a citation was the result of driving too fast until January 2019, when she received one from the New York State Assembly for Distinguished Educational & Human Rights Services for her work in promoting LGBTQ+ rights and inclusion. *The Savvy Ally* is her first book. Visit her website and download free informational handouts at www.savvyallyaction.com.